# IN THE BOTTOM 1%
## THE CHALLENGE OF REFORMING A FAILED URBAN SCHOOL

BRAD GRANT
HISTORY TEACHER
LINCOLN HIGH SCHOOL
MIDWEST CITY
©2016

## DISCLAIMER

Lincoln High School is a real high school in a real Midwestern city of about 150,000 people. I am a History teacher at that school. For the purposes of this book I have renamed everything – the city, the school, the staff, and the students. Other than the names, everything in this book happened at Lincoln High School between the years of 2010 and 2016. Most of the stories take place during my first year as a teacher in the building, but some background information is from before my time. If I wasn't present for an event, I interviewed those involved for the details, or in the case of a fight, I watched the videos that students posted on YouTube. The purpose of these stories is to reveal the true conditions in urban schools in the US while protecting the identities of those involved.

*(The cover photo of this book is a manipulated version of a picture of Lincoln Park High School in Chicago, IL taken by Vernes Seferovic. It is in no way related to this book, despite the similarity in name.)*

I was hired at Lincoln High after the teacher in my position quit the day before school started because of "working conditions." That should have been a warning sign. Lincoln High was a school in failure. In my first month of work I saw students drop out and teachers quit, I was involved in gang brawls in the hallway, and I saw worse test scores than I ever thought possible. Lincoln High was in the bottom one percent of all high schools in the state. From my first year to my fourth year at LHS, the staff and many students attempted to turnaround the school. With help from an eight million dollar grant and a new administration, the school slowly began to improve.

## SCHOOL INTRO

Lincoln High has a long history as a successful school. The building is around 100 years old and is situated in the middle of a neighborhood in the oldest part of Midwest City. The school keeps a Hall of Fame in the Commons with a long list of significant graduates from the past. Based on the Hall of Fame the school seems very impressive, but the Hall doesn't have any members under the age of 40 that aren't athletes. The school hasn't had a famous graduate in politics, literature, law, science, or social studies since before 1990. Since then we have produced a few NBA players, but not much else. This is a symptom of changing demographics in Midwest City that have moved a lot of students to other high schools in the area. The district also has a school choice program that allows academically gifted students to apply for another high school in the district and take college level Upper Placement (UP) and Worldwide Baccalaureate (WB) classes.

Around 2004, the school started a decline that would lead to it reaching the bottom of the state's high school rankings list. Over 20,000 referrals were being written by teachers each school year, the graduation rate was below 60%, the attendance rate was below 70%, and crime was rampant in the hallways. In 2008 another failing high school in the district was merged with Lincoln High, causing complete chaos in the school. Rival street gangs were now forced to attend the same school, and the police had to be called into the building constantly for issues that it caused.

The school hit rock bottom in the 2010-2011 school year. Late in the school year a teacher compiled a report on the failures, standardized test scores, discipline, student attendance, drop-outs, and teacher attendance at the school. The report revealed that almost nothing of academic value was happening at Lincoln High. In the summer of 2011 it was decided that a major turnaround needed to take place at the school. A new principal was selected - Mr. Everett. He met with a core group of teachers early in the summer and began the work of fixing the school. The district gave Mr. Everett free reign on hiring that summer. He wiped the slate clean in the administration and brought in four new assistant principals. He also was given the ability to release 50% of the teaching staff, which he did. Dozens of new teachers were brought in - either successful teachers from around the district or new hires fresh out of college. The core group of teachers and Mr. Everett then began work on an application for a grant. The school was awarded a three year eight million dollar grant for school improvement. The team used the rest of the summer to decide how to spend the money. It was decided that all teachers at Lincoln High would be using a new style of instruction in 2011. The plan put into place revolved around teacher-student relationships, standards based planning, and engagement strategies.

When students arrived for the 2011-2012 school year, they were greeted with a new level of energy from the staff at Lincoln High. Most of them were used to the old ways, so there was major resistance in the first couple of years. I was hired at the start of the 2012 school year during the second year of the turnaround. The plan was still in the early stages, and there was still major student resistance all year. The last group of students from the old system graduated in 2014, and it was only until we had an entirely new group of students that we saw any changes.

## PART 1 - THE FALL

A school can fail for dozens of reasons. Funding can be cut, administrators can ignore needs, teachers can fail to adapt, students can stop caring, crime can invade the building, parents can be bad role models, demographics can change, and communities can become plagued with violence. A good school could deal with one or two of these problems. A strong school in a violent neighborhood could still produce good results. A strong staff could find ways to engage students who don't care. Lincoln High failed because all of these issues began around 2004 and only got worse as time went on.

## STUDENTS

**Demographics**

Lincoln High is a school of about 1500 students. The number has fluctuated over the years, and student mobility has made it difficult to track, but the number has stayed around 1500 for ten or more years. 70% of the school population is black, 15% is white, 10% are Hispanic, and the remaining students are spread thinly through other categories. Over 80% of the students are from low income families and between 15-20% have some form of learning disability. During the failure of LHS, the school's 4 year graduate rate was 50%, and student attendance was below 70%.

One of the more alarming statistics at Lincoln High is teen pregnancy. Midwest County has more teen pregnancies than any county in the United States. Of my 150 students in a given school year, at least 20 of them are either parents or soon to be parents. One future pregnant student even stated, "You can't get welfare without a baby, so you might as well have one."

Some of these numbers have no effect on school performance, but combining the data creates a picture of a school filled with problems.

**School Culture**

20,000 office referrals were written in the 2010-2011 school year.  The behavior of students at Lincoln High was unlike any other school in the area.  If you spent a day at Lincoln High you would see things that wouldn't and couldn't happen at any other high school.  A school day started at 8am with first hour.  Students arrived by bus and on foot, with a few drivers.  Less than half of the students made it on time to first hour.  If you stood by the student entrance at 8:00 you would see a huge line of students waiting to get a tardy pass from a secretary.  Students trickled in slowly up to 10:30am.

After watching students arrive late you could observe a few classes.  In most classes you would see about 30 students crammed in to tiny classrooms built before World War 2.  In a room of 30 less than 5 of the students would be doing any work.  Most teachers would be sitting at their desk reading or looking at the computer.  They would start class by passing out a packet of worksheets and then returning to their seat.  Most kids wouldn't do any of the work, but teachers didn't really care as long as they stayed in their seats and didn't do anything too crazy.

If teachers didn't really care it made no sense for them to write 20,000 referrals, but they still did. They would write up everything that happened in the course of a class period without really even trying to stop the behaviors on their own. If a student had a cell phone out, teachers would just write an electronics referral instead of asking for them to put it away. If students were talking loudly and cussing, they would just be sent out with a referral. There were rarely any attempts made by teachers to stop the behaviors that were happening, so they continued.

A passing period at Lincoln High didn't have a lot of movement. Students would file out of class and gather in huge crowds blocking the hallways. There would be no sense of urgency to make it to the next class. Girls would scream down the hallways to their friends and boys would drop F-bombs and N-bombs as loud as possible. A fight might break out, and if it did everyone nearby would rush to get a view. The bell would ring for the next class to start, and then the students would start moving.

The lunchroom was where the action happened. Almost every day there was a fight at lunch in the Commons. Some were loud shouting matches, others were short one on one fights, but some days huge groups of students would brawl.  After every lunch period the Commons would be strewn with garbage left behind by the students.  A lot of them would leave the building directly from lunch, but there were two more classes that they were supposed to attend.

At the end of every day there was a rush for the Commons.  Students wanted to see if a fight would happen, and that was the usual meeting place.  If there was no fight disappointed students would eventually make their way out of the building, but could hopefully catch one on the walk home in the parking lot of nearby businesses.

To say the least, Lincoln High was a rough school.  There was more misbehavior happening than there was learning.

**Disruption and Insubordination**

20,000 referrals for 1500 students - that is an extreme amount of referrals.  Some students could go an entire year without getting a referral, but others had over 50 a year.  A handful of students had over 100 referrals in a single school year.

Most referrals are not for violence or criminal activity.  Most referrals are either for cutting class,

disrupting class, or being insubordinate.  Disruptions were a constant problem at Lincoln High.  Students would sit in class blasting music from their headphones and having personal conversations at full volume while teachers tried to teach.  Some teachers could keep a class entertained long enough to teach a short lesson, but only after assuring students they would have time to talk at the end.  If the disruptions got too loud, teachers would ask the students to see their dean.  Students who willingly left would receive disruption referrals.  Students who refused to leave and created even more of a scene would need to be escorted out by security.  Teachers would place a call and wait a few minutes for security to arrive.  These students would receive insubordination referrals.  The behavior behind both referrals was the same, and it was a constant problem at Lincoln High.
 Disruptions and Insubordination were major issues, but they didn't give Lincoln High its reputation like fighting did.

**Minor Fights**

Lincoln High was known as a fighting school. In my first two years in the building I was witness to more fights than I can remember. LHS had more fights in a week than most schools have in an entire year. Girls would build up drama for days before the fighting started, and boys would claim rival gang membership so they could fight in the halls. The following are just some examples of the day to day fights that occurred at LHS that I was involved in.

Monique vs. Ally

Girl fights are always the most dangerous to break up. Girls fight at a level of intensity that is far beyond most boy fights. A lot of boys who fight at school do it for attention or because they know adults will step in before anything major happens. Girls fight at school because they physically can't wait until after school. When two girls with a problem see each other they have to fight, not matter where they are. As an adult stepping in to break up a girl fight you can be guaranteed that you will be resisted and you will most likely end up scratched or punched.

Monique and Ally were juniors with a long standing beef. Their beef started on Twitter, moved to Facebook, and eventually made it to the lunch room.  A few weeks prior to the beef Monique had been seen talking to the ex-boyfriend of Ally's cousin.  Ally's cousin Destiny began the beef by talking trash about Monique and her ex-boyfriend on Twitter.  The first post began an all-night comment war involving several girls but mostly led by Ally.  The drama built outside of school unknown to teachers, principals, or security.  When the drama had finally reached a point where no one could identify the real reason for the argument or use logic to end it, it erupted into a fight in the Commons during lunch.

   I was walking down the stairs into the Commons when I heard shrieking girls and the roar of a crowd.  As I rounded the corner into the Commons I ran into a wall of students.  On the other side of the wall Ally and Monique were locked in life and death combat.  Both girls were holding each other by the hair with one hand while swinging wildly with the other.  Dozens of punches landed before I was able to break through the crowd.  As I reached the two girls they were standing with their heads down while still gripping each other's hair.  They were locked together like two bucks who stuck their horns after a head-butting session.  I tried to place my body between them while grabbing Ally and pulling her back but Monique would not let go.  Only after I grabbed Monique's wrist was I able to unlock them from each other.  I pushed Ally back about 10 feet, but she continued squirming and trying to escape me.  No other adult had arrived, so Monique was free to give chase as I tried to remove Ally.  Ally broke free of my sloppy wrist lock and tried to push into Monique, but I was able to get between them again.  As I was pushing Ally back again she began trying to reach over me to punch Monique.  This didn't really work.  I'm fairly large - 6'6" 225lbs - and the girls were fairly small - around 5'5" 115lbs.  All of Ally's attempts to punch over me ended up landing on my shoulder instead.  As Ally was attempting these punches other adults finally arrived and dragged away Monique.

   I walked Ally up to a principal's office to wait for backup.  It was only after the fight had calmed that I realized the true damage done in the fight.  Ally appeared to have a broken nose and a gash on her forehead.  Monique's wild punches had done some extreme damage.  Ally's nose was dripping blood like a faucet and had gotten all over my shirt.  I went to my gym bag for a change of clothes and continued on to lunch.  As I passed by the site of the fight everything was calm as if nothing had happened.  The only evidence of a fight was a large pile of weave blowing around the floor like tumbleweed.  Tumbleweave was a frequent sight after a girl fight at Lincoln High.

AFTERMATH

-Ally had her nose repaired and returned to school after her suspension.  She didn't get into any fights after the incident, but she was suspended for cussing out several of her teachers.

-Monique returned from her suspension and continued on as if nothing had happened.  She maintained decent grades despite her suspension for fighting.

-Destiny attempted to continue the drama by threatening to fight Monique's friends during the suspensions of Ally and Monique.  She was given a short suspension as well and decided to take an extra ten days off of school.  Her grades suffered the most out of the three girls because of her extended stay at home.

Jasmine vs. Brionna

Jasmine was what we refer to as a "frequent flyer." Despite being a senior, she was constantly kicked out of classes, roaming the halls, in In School Suspension, or on the Saturday morning detention list. She and her friends would intentionally roam the halls screaming and shouting during classes just to disrupt things. Her goal every school day was to cause as much disruption as possible.

Brionna had a history of discipline issues, but most were as a freshman. She had been in fights before, but she had declared her "retirement" from fighting and was trying to focus on academics. By her senior year she was actually on track to graduate and had recovered her missing credits from freshman year.

These two girls were not a good mix. Jasmine wanted to disrupt everything, and Brionna wanted to take school seriously, but could easily revert to her past self.

Mr. Zachary taught senior Economics and was a very dry lecturer who required almost absolute silence from his students. But as the day progressed, he became worn down by his Friday classes that were becoming more rowdy by the hour. By 8th hour he was done correcting or kicking out students. Jasmine often found herself ejected from Mr. Zachary's 8th hour, but today he attempted to ignore her. She was loudly having a conversation during an assignment and was annoying the majority of the class. Brionna was a ticking time bomb that Jasmine didn't realize was about to explode. After she had finally had enough, Brionna stood up and shouted at Jasmine. She gave a minute long passionate speech about Jasmine's lack of seriousness and inability to complete any school work. Before she reached her conclusion, Jasmine got up from her seat, charged Brionna, and started swinging.

Like an Old West saloon brawl, Mr. Zachary's classroom door flung open with force and the two girls landed in a pile in the hallway. Jasmine's momentum carried her and Brionna through the slightly ajar door and into the hallway. The force of the blow was enough to shatter the safety glass on the door, but it wasn't enough to stop Brionna. Brionna looked like an MMA fighter as she trapped Jasmine on the floor and began pummeling her.

My classroom was at a major T-intersection in the hallway that usually gave me a good view of anything happening on the 2nd floor. I was teaching my 8th hour when I heard an extremely loud crash and shattering noise. Out of my door window I saw Jasmine and Brionna engaged in a ground wrestling match. I came out of my classroom and walked down to the brawl. There's no easy approach to breaking up a ground fight, and I definitely wasn't going down to the ground with them. I grabbed Jasmine under the armpits and tried to lift her off the ground, but Brionna's grip was so strong that I ended up just dragging them both 5 feet down the hallway. By this time Mr. Zachary's entire class had emptied into the hallway, and two boys from his class helped break them apart. They were both winded from their wrestling match and chose to stay on the floor until officers arrived.

AFTERMATH

> -Brionna went on the graduate on time and was not suspended again the rest of her school career.
>
> -Jasmine returned from her suspension and began a streak of major disruptions that eventually led to her expulsion and placement at a district alternative school. She was not seen at Lincoln High again after this. Her

major disruptions are covered in the Major Incidents chapter.

Cedric and Tyler vs. Dashaun

Real gang members don't really attend school. They sometimes register as part of court ordered school attendance, but most of them stop coming after a couple of days. On some rare occasions two rival gang members will be registered and a fight will result. The real problem at Lincoln High is wannabee gang bangers. Students who think they are hard because they listen to terrible local rap and smoke weed like to claim allegiance to the street gangs in town.

Cedric, Tyler, and Dashaun were seniors by age (though none of them had senior credits) who were all friends from the same neighborhood. Cedric was an amateur rapper who had recently released a few videos on YouTube. Tyler and Dashaun were his hype men. They appeared in the videos smoking and moving around in the background, but didn't have Cedric's rapping talent. Naturally, Cedric became the group leader. In one song the three claimed gang membership by shouting "gang" dozens of times throughout the track, but in reality they were not street gang criminals. The only crimes they ever committed were misdemeanor street fights, and besides Tyler's stint in rehab for marijuana, none of them had ever been incarcerated. Early in their senior year the boys had a falling out. Dashaun was seen on a "diss-track" YouTube video that talked trash on Cedric and Tyler. This began the beef that eventually led to an attempted attack on Dashaun at school.

One morning in September Cedric and Tyler arrived at school together and were seen hanging out with a large crowd in the Commons before 1st hour. This was a rarity because Tyler almost never attended school, and when he did he was never on time. An assistant principal walking through the Commons heard Tyler say, "let me know when you are doing it and I'll leave class." The body language of the group was obvious - a fight was about to happen.

Dashaun's 1st hour class - Psychology - was on the 2nd floor just up the stairs from the Commons. His teacher, Mrs. Zook, was talking with some of her students as others were filing in to start class. Mrs. Zook, despite her history as a college basketball player, was small in comparison to most students, and was pregnant at the time. Cedric and Tyler took this as their opportunity to get revenge on Dashaun.

As they entered the classroom, Mrs. Zook recognized and greeted them, but asked what they were doing in her room so early as they didn't have her class until 5th hour. They ignored her greeting and pushed by her towards Dashaun. Dashaun saw them coming, but no words were exchanged before Cedric began swinging on him. The two assumed boxing stances and began pummeling each other as the other students tried to get out of the way.

Mr. Sheridan, the assistant principal from the Commons hustled up the stairs following Cedric and Tyler. He had just gotten to work, so he didn't have a radio on him to call for backup. He entered Mrs. Zook's room as the fight was starting. Mr. Sheridan entered the fight by attempting to grab Cedric, but Tyler (a 300 pounder) was boxing him out. Cedric and Dashaun continued fighting while Tyler bulldozed all of the desks to the walls. Mr. Sheridan got a hand on Cedric, but could not stop a 3 man fight. Mrs. Zook, realizing that backup was not on the way, ran to my room to get help.

As I entered Mrs. Zook's room, I saw Mr. Sheridan pressed against the back corner of the room trying to hold Cedric in an arm lock. Dashaun was still throwing punches and Cedric was half broken free from Mr. Sheridan's grip. Tyler was circling the fight and throwing the occasional cheap shot at Dashaun's side. I shoved by the students blocking the doorway to the room and grabbed Dashaun in a bear hug around the shoulders. He continued try to fight, so I turned him and put him chest first onto a desktop.

With Dashaun and Cedric under control, Tyler tried to get a few cheap shots in, so I tried to drag Dashaun out of the room. It would've ended there, but when I got to the doorway my path was blocked by four 19-20 year olds who had trespassed into the building to watch the fight. Two of them were former students who had dropped out the previous school year, but the other two were just random people off the street.

With the inclusion of the trespassers into the incident it became a police issue instead of a school issue. The four intruders tried to run but were arrested outside of the school.

AFTERMATH

>-Cedric dropped out of school and is presumably continuing his amateur rap career on the streets of Midwest City.

-Tyler was dropped from school for having too many absences. He is most likely still working as Cedric's hype man, and probably relapsed on marijuana.

-Dashaun returned to Lincoln High but was forced to take a 5$^{th}$ year of high school to make up for missing credits.

-The four trespasser students were fined for trespassing and have since appeared in the county commitment report several times.

Brandy and Caleb vs. Monte

Girl fights were passionate, and boy fights always involved heavy hitting, but the ultimate form of fighting was boy vs. girl group fights. If a boy and a girl got into an argument the idea of "never hit a girl" didn't cross the boy's mind. Boy vs. girl fights were seen as acceptable, but they would usually involve another boy or another girl jumping in to even the odds.

Monte's face was frequently seen on the county jail commitment report. He was a 19 year old senior just scraping by in his classes. Most days in class he would just sit in a corner and do nothing, but he had to be at school because of a court order.

Brandy was a senior girl who loved to argue. She had a short fuse and would get in anyone's face for the slightest infractions. She shared a math class with Monte. One day early in the school year Brandy was arguing in math class with Curtis, a male student in the class. Brandy accused Curtis of trying to "hook up" with her over text message the previous night. The argument got loud and the teacher, Mrs. Cole, didn't intervene to stop it. At this point Monte had had enough. He told Brandy to "shut the fuck up" and that he was tired of hearing her voice all the time. Brandy, already with adrenaline flowing from her argument with Curtis, wasted no time. She cussed out Monte and stormed out of the room with a promise to return.

Brandy ran two rooms down to Mr. Zachary's room, where her brother Caleb was in his Government class. She told Caleb to get up and follow her back to her class. The brother and sister team returned to Mrs. Cole's room and immediately jumped Monte. Monte barely had enough time to stand up before the fighting started. Monte had been to jail and he knew how the fight and Caleb liked to box in his neighborhood, so they both could handle themselves. Brandy brought her signature brand of crazy into the mix and the results destroyed Mrs. Cole's room.  This wasn't a fight that you crowd around to watch; this was a fight that you run away from so you don't end up knocked out.  The other students from the classroom cleared out into the hallway as fast as possible to avoid the brawl.  Every teacher on the floor heard the crashing desks and screams from the fight, but no one could even try to step in.  I usually have no problem stepping into a fight, but I could only watch this one.

   On this day we had four armed campus police officers and one city police detective in the building.  It took all five of them to stop Brandy, Caleb, and Monte.  The campus officers stormed into the room and slammed into the fighters.  Two officers took Caleb into a wall and tried to cuff him.  One officer took Monte to the floor and another tried to corral Brandy.  The detective did not step in because she didn't want to escalate the fight into a city police problem.  All three fighters continued resisting and breaking free of the officers, so one of them got out their mace and started spraying the fighters. Monte was maced, and he finally stopped resisting.  The officers were able to cuff Caleb as well, but Brandy found a way to slip out of the room and run away.

She hid in a bathroom for about five minutes biding her time. The boys were separated and sent to separate offices to receive their suspensions while security searched for Brandy on the security cameras. After five minutes Brandy came out of the bathroom and stormed down to the main office. The city detective saw her coming and told her to stop. Brandy entered the office anyway and started screaming - demanding to see Monte so she could continue the fight. She made it into the principal's secretary's office when the detective gave her final warning. Brandy ignored the detective one last time, so Detective Barker pulled out her taser and shot Brandy, bringing her to the ground. She was cuffed and arrested.

AFTERMATH

>   -Brandy made bail and was back at school after an extended suspension. She actually graduated and now works at a Subway in town. I've seen her a few times since graduation and she is always very friendly, so she must have matured.
> 
>   -Caleb was also arrested for leaving one classroom to commit assault in another. Hc was also charged with resisting for the

extreme fight he put up against the school police. He returned from his long suspension, but fought again and was eventually expelled.
-Monte returned from his suspension briefly, but soon moved to Chicago and wasn't seen again in Midwest City. He got involved with a gang in Chicago and was shot and killed in a street fight about a year later.

Other Fights

These incidents all qualify as "minor" fights at Lincoln High. Most schools would probably call a fight involving mace and tasers as major incidents that would probably make the news, but not in Midwest City. There were dozens of minor fights like this at Lincoln High in my first couple of years as a teacher. I personally broke up ten fights in my first year, and there were around one hundred total fights.

Keamber jumped Ameerah at an assembly and broke a teacher's glasses in the process.

Tariah fought her ex-boyfriend Armand in the cafeteria on top of the tables.

Kylesha fought her own sister Kynesha in a class they shared.

Kya fought De'Asia in a planned bathroom fight that they broke up on their own afterwards.

Lexus fought Andesha in the Commons and punched me when I tried to break it up.

Traveon fought Kendric and had to be put in a choke hold by his teacher to make him stop.

Demetrio and Alonzo fought, were suspended, and fought again the day they got back.

Deontray fought Khalil because Khalil accidently hit Deontray on the head with a desk he was moving.

Trey fought James on the first day of school while waiting to register for classes - not even technically students yet.

Alonzo one punch knocked out Hermes because "he wouldn't shut up talking."

Bayley got in a fight while pregnant and shoved me when I tried to break it up.

Shawndeja fought Kenneth because they were arguing about who won a fight earlier in the day.

A very special ed student Jasmine fought Derek and tried to fight the pregnant assistant principal who broke it up.

Darius fought Kayla and then screamed the name of a gang 25 times as he was being dragged to the office.

Destiny fought Alaina in the cafeteria while security was responding to a fight on the 3rd floor.  It was broken up by a janitor and a Navy recruiter.  The janitor's phone was stolen during the fight by someone in the crowd.

Different freshmen girls fought outside the Commons every day for 6 straight days until the school threatened to arrest the next 2 girls that fought.

Rayven jumped Krista as she exited her science class and took two teachers to the floor.

Jontasia (250 lb.) fought Dominique (275 lb.) and jumped on the assistant principal's back who tried to break it up.  He had to have surgery.

Jaylan fought Jordan in the library, and intentionally flipped a table full of computers to start the show.

Jada jumped Shakyra and got several solid punches to Shakyra's face.  Some senior boys broke up the fight, but when Shakyra's friend Selena arrived it all started again.  Selena pushed Jada out the side door of the building, threw her on the ground, and beat her until she was restrained.

Fast Food Fights

It's a long standing tradition among boys at Lincoln High to fight in the parking lots of the local fast food restaurants a few blocks from the school. Girls fight at school all the time, but only about half of the boy fights happen in the building. A lot of boys put their fights in their daily schedule and plan to meet in the McDonald's parking lot at 2:40 or the KFC parking lot at 2:45, depending on which direction they usually walk home. Teachers and school security don't break these fights up or even see most of them; they are a city police issue. In most situations no arrests are made because everyone scatters if police arrive. The school can still suspend students for fighting on the way home from school though, and will if they hear about it or see video evidence.

Drake and Arion were seniors that were not on track to graduate. They were both classified as juniors and were facing a fifth year if they didn't get their acts together. Both of them transferred to a credit recovery school in the district for potential fifth years to earn more credits. Arion was doing fine in the program at the Adams Center, but Drake was a behavior problem. He refused to listen to the teachers in his credit recovery program and constantly disrupted his classes. At Adams the staff doesn't really deal with discipline. Students that disrupt are just sent home, and constant behavior problems will just result in being dropped and sent back to the original school. Drake was sent back to Lincoln High for his behavior. Arion just couldn't live without his friend Drake, so even though he was on track to graduate on time he decided to transfer back to Lincoln High as well.

Travon was a junior with freshman credits. He had never passed an academic class in his three years at Lincoln High. His current grades were straight F's, even in PE. What should have been impossible for a student with good attendance was made possible by Travon.

Travon and Drake began a week-long feud over social media and in person at school. No one really knows the origins of the argument, but they were probably arguing about who was least likely to graduate. The debate came to a boil one Wednesday after school in the Commons. Travon and Drake began a shouting match about who could beat whose ass. Travon told Drake to meet him outside where a fight was supposed to happen. Because of the major scene they caused in the Commons they were already surrounded by security when they arrived outside and a fight was avoided. Sadly, because they never actually fought they couldn't legally be suspended from school.

The next day everyone knew a fight was going to happen. The extra day allowed both Drake and Travon to plan for it and gather supporters. Drake found his friend Arion and another friend Kewan. Kewan also recruited his 22 year old cousin to their side. Travon found Juan and 3 other friends. The anticipation was so great that they couldn't handle waiting until the end of school to fight, so they texted each other and agreed to walk out of the building in the middle of the day and meet at KFC. Between 3rd and 4th hour they all snuck out of different doors and walked the two blocks to KFC. Kewan's older cousin was there waiting for them. Drake also brought a friend to document their activities, Reggie. Reggie recorded everything from the exiting of the building to the arrival at KFC and the fight.

No one really knew how to start a large 5 on 5 brawl, so when they all met at KFC they mostly milled around the parking lot giving dirty looks to each other. Finally, Drake decided to start things off by going after Juan, the smallest member of the other party. Drake approached Juan and grabbed his shoulder. He demanded that Juan give him his phone and wallet to avoid being beat up. Drake grabbed Juan's phone, but Juan held on to it until Kewan's cousin stepped in. The 22 year old man with apparently nothing better to do on a Thursday morning threw one punch at Juan and knocked him out cold. Drake then grabbed Jose's phone before the brawl began. Travon and his posse tried to jump in and gain back momentum, but the presence of an adult made it impossible. Soon all of Travon and his friends were on the ground being kicked over and over by Drake and his posse. After a few minutes of kicking the fight was declared over and everyone limped away.

Reggie, like many other Lincoln High teens, was not the best decision maker. Most people who record their friends committing crimes would think to destroy or delete the evidence of the crime so as to avoid police involvement. Reggie apparently didn't think of this. Instead, he went to work on his computer editing the footage. He made some cuts, added music, and even added slow motion replays of the greatest hits from the fight. After completing his work he then uploaded it to his public Facebook page for everyone at school to see. By 7th hour hundreds of students had seen the fight that took place during 4th hour outside of the building. By 8th hour security and principals had seen the fight as well and alerted the city police.

After school, a large group of girls gathered in the Commons. They were friends of Drake, Arion, Kewan, Reggie, Travon, and Juan and they had all seen the fight video from earlier in the day. Passionate supporters of Juan decided to get revenge by fighting the girlfriends of the boys from the other side. This all out brawl between six girls proved that fighting is the only solution to problems that many students can think of.

AFTERMATH

>    -Drake was arrested for assault after the video was seen by Midwest City police. He eventually returned to school, but did not graduate on time.

-Arion returned to school after his extended suspension, but like Drake did not graduate on time.

-Reggie received a short suspension for walking out of the building, but didn't fight anyone so was not given a full five days. He still has the video up on his Facebook to this day.

-Kewan returned from his suspension and gained respect from many students for his performance in the fight. He was not seen as someone capable of fighting until after the video was released. He enjoyed the respect and attention so much that he decided to take a 5th year of high school.

-Travon returned from his long suspension and continued doing what he always did - setting Lincoln High records for most F's earned.

-Juan returned to school and got his phone back. Besides being knocked out he suffered the least from the fight.

-Kewan's cousin was arrested for fighting teenagers and was probably beaten up in jail by a 28 year old.

## Major Incidents

The KFC fight between Drake and Travon was the worst incident in the minor category of fights. While it involved 9 students walking out of school, an assault, a robbery, a 22 year old, a girlfriend retaliatory brawl, and a couple of arrests, it doesn't match up to the major incidents that took place at Lincoln High in my first 2 years at the school. A minor fight is simple - it involves students fighting. It could be destructive or they could get arrested, but the fight is still minor unless it disrupts the entire school. Several events occurred in my years at Lincoln High that caused disruptions so large that most of the school was involved.

Gang Wars Day

Gangs have been mostly removed from Lincoln High. The administration and campus police have gotten very good at identifying members and having them removed before anything happens. This was not the case in previous years. Gang affiliated students roamed the halls in my first few months at Lincoln High. Most of them didn't go to many classes; they just sort of roamed around and congregated in hard to find deserted corners of the building.

Tay was an 18 year old junior, one year behind in credits. He was also a legitimate gang member with a criminal record. He was only attending school because he was required to as a condition of his probation. He had a few friends, some gang members and some wannabees, that would follow him around school all day. Jarvis, Jameel, and Montel were three of his groupies.

Kalvin was a senior and a member of a rival gang in Midwest City. He had spent most of his high school career in Juvenile Detention, but over the summer he was released and required to register as a senior at LHS. He had several junior and sophomore followers, just like Tay.

On a Monday night in September two rival gangs had a street fight in a neighborhood near the school. Several of the people involved were adults, but Tay's cousin and Kalvin were both present at the fight. Kalvin and his fellow gang members severely beat Tay's cousin that night.

The next morning at school, the bells stopped working. I was in the halls ushering students to class when I noticed Tay and a group of nine other boys in an animated discussion with each other.  Their body language said that they were looking for someone, and judging by their demeanor they were clearly trying to fight whoever they found.  I thought I could stop what was about to happen, so I followed them.  Because I was a rookie, I didn't call anyone for backup, I just strolled behind them to see where they were going.  A large group of students also noticed Tay's attitude and thought the same thing I did, so more than 50 of them followed as well.

Tay and his group went downstairs to the 1st floor and met up with a large group of Kalvin and his friends.  Kalvin had a dozen friends with him and over 200 students from the Commons had followed them.  At this point I was the only adult anywhere near the two groups, but others were starting to notice and make calls to security.  Students from the crowd pulled out their phones and started recording because they knew what was about to happen.

I stepped between Tay and Kalvin and tried to raise my voice above them to make them stop, but I was drowned out by the roar of the massive crowd that was still growing.  I was able to prevent Tay and Kalvin from fighting, but their groups were too large.  Jameel squared off with a boy from Kalvin's group and started the brawl. Within seconds there were six separate boxing matches in the same hallway. The rest of the supporters from both sides charged into the fray and created a pile of fighting gangbangers. Girls were swinging purses into the pile trying to hit their boyfriends' rivals, boys were jumping in from out of nowhere and creating a bigger mess, and dozens of bystanders there for the show were being shoved into the lockers and down onto the floor.

No adult response could have been fast enough or large enough to stop this brawl. I was the only teacher in the middle of the crowd, but there were several others trying to push through to the middle. I entered the melee and grabbed the first swinging participant I could get my hands on. From behind me two fighters rammed into my back and I went down to the floor, taking a fighter with me. I landed with my knees on top of the fighter I had grabbed and just held on until it was over. From behind me I felt the fighters who had rammed me punching me in the back trying to reach someone under me, so I threw back an arm and grabbed ahold of whoever was hitting me. The football coach and an aide, both over 300 pounds, then arrived and jumped into the pile. Soon the security guards and the police arrived to corral everyone. Every adult grabbed a fighter and tried to force them to stop. I took the boy who punched me in back and grabbed him in a bear hug. He resisted, and because I was full of adrenaline I slammed him into a locker and yelled at him as loud as I could. The fight was over, but it was only 1st hour, and the problems of that day were just starting.

After the 20 student brawl the adults began a long process of sorting out what happened. Security was outnumbered, so they called in city police. City police arrived and students were divided into manageable groups. Each student was handcuffed and processed by assistant principals. With so many students involved, the priority was making sure everyone was suspended that was involved. On top of being suspended, most of the students were arrested for mob action and taken away in police paddy wagons. By the end of 1st hour the students were processed and removed from the building.

In the chaos of the fight a lot of involved students got away. By the time 1st hour ended they had all made their way to their classes, and probably thought they had gotten away with it. The assistant principals were trying to check camera footage for remaining fighters when 1st hour ended. Students moved to the halls again to head to 2nd hour. Jarvis, one of the original fighters, had escaped from suspension and arrest, and was back in the hallway. He was spotted by some of Kalvin's friends who were also involved and the brawl began again in the Commons. This time, the adult response was faster, but five more students fought and were suspended. The halls were cleared after an extra-long passing period, and finally everyone made it to 2nd hour. Once the halls were cleared the principal came on the intercom and announced a "soft lockdown." This meant that we would have class as usual, but we would hold in 2nd hour until we heard otherwise.

    The city police came in force to the building. Officers in groups of 4 were stationed at every corner of the hallways and came armed with batons for crowd control. The district sent all available campus security from other schools and called in 2nd shift security early. The building was packed with officers by the time we were ready to release for 3rd hour. Students in 2nd hour were simmering. During soft lockdown they developed an imprisoned mentality and their rage increased. When the principal came on to announce we were moving to 3rd hour, a near riot began on the 3rd floor. Any student who had an issue with any other student on the 3rd floor decided it was time to settle it.  Even those who weren't fighting took part in the chaos by screaming and running up and down the halls.  Quintez, a boy with long dreads, got in a fight with Adrian, and had a dread ripped out.  Lamell, a freshman, grabbed the loose dead and ran up and down the hall swinging it in circles while screaming.  Cleveland, another freshman, threatened to fight his English teacher if she wouldn't let him into the hall to join the fighting.

  The police finally settled everyone down and we got 3rd hour underway.  Dozens more students were suspended, but most of them managed to get away.  We held in 3rd hour for double the normal length as police and security searched room by room for anyone involved and had them removed.  We missed 4th hour entirely and sent the students to 5th after a warning that any further problems would result in automatic arrest for anyone involved.  We somehow managed to make it through the rest of the day without another incident, probably because everyone even remotely involved had been carted out of the building already.  The day is still the record holder for most suspensions in one day at Lincoln High.

AFTERMATH

- All of the major fighters from the first fight were put up for expulsion. They were suspended until their hearings and were sent to alternative schools within the district.
- The major fighters from the second and third fights were given 10 day suspensions - the maximum length other than expulsion.
- The fringe / minor fighters from the first, second, and third fights were given five day suspensions - the standard length for a fight.
- The major disruptors who never fought were given staggered in-school suspensions throughout the rest of that week.
- The LHS administration worked with the police to set up a system that allowed us to recognize gang members before anything like this could happen again.

Walkout Brawls

Jasmine and Terrance were the leading disruptors in the school.  Jasmine was previously involved in the Old West style saloon fight in Mr. Zachary's room, and returned from her suspension louder than ever.  She would spend every passing period roaming the halls screaming with her friends, and always tried to instigate drama.  Terrance could best be described as flamboyant.  He followed around Jasmine and her girlfriends hoping they would get involved in some drama.  He would be the first person at every fight scene with his phone out so he could record it and upload it to Facebook.

Jasmine and her crew got word that a fight was supposed to happen at some point during the school day.  They didn't know who it was supposed to involve, they just knew that something was brewing somewhere.  Terrance whipped out his phone and started recording, and Jasmine and her crew started circling the hallways gathering a crowd.  They rounded the 2nd floor but couldn't find what they were looking for, so they took their huge crowd to the first floor.  By this point they were all jogging, which attracted the attention of hundreds of students who joined in.  Adults all over the building noticed the parade of clowns running by their rooms, and about half followed to try to return them all to class.

Eventually the crowd reached the Commons where they found what they were looking for. Shakyra, a freshman, was fighting against another freshman Star. When the crowd arrived, Star's boyfriend Demond entered the fight and threw Shakyra on the ground. Once he had her on the floor he started kicking her in the face repeatedly. The mass chaos started by Jasmine made it impossible to reach the fight and stop Demond, so Shakyra ended up with a busted open lip and needed stitches on her face. More than half of the school was out of the classrooms at this point, so they had to be herded back by the rest of the teachers.

AFTERMATH

> -Jasmine was finally expelled and sent to an alternative school for her major disruptions.
> -Terrance was suspended, but he got his video on Facebook.
> -Shakyra returned to school, got in several more fights, and got pregnant, but eventually graduated.

The Down Low

Cory was a deep-voiced junior who carefully created an image as a tough guy.  He was actually very smart and was doing well in most of his classes despite the image.  His girlfriend Aniah was also a junior in several Honors classes.  They both stayed out of trouble for the most part, though they did smoke weed outside of school.

Ray, like Terrance before him, was one of the most flamboyant guys in the school.  He wore leggings to school every day so everyone could see everything.  He earned the nickname "Moose Knuckle" as he pranced down the hallway talking loudly with a fake lisp.

In the afternoon on a mid-February day, Ray and Cory were involved in one of the most extreme non-gang related dramas to ever take place at Lincoln High.  During the lunch hours rumors began flying around the school that Cory and Ray had secretly created a sex tape and that Cory had paid Ray $300 for what took place on the video.  Ray let the word slip to some girls who let other girls know, and by the end of the lunch periods the entire school was talking.

Word got to Cory pretty quickly, and as he ate lunch he became angrier and angrier every time someone said something to him.  When the bell rang Cory stormed out of the cafeteria and went up to the 2nd floor where Ray was in class.  The entire cafeteria followed him with their phones already recording.  Cory reached Ray's class and began screaming into the doorway that he was going to "beat his ass after school."  Another teacher and I blocked the doorway to the classroom while Ray taunted Cory from inside.  The crowd grew, but Cory could not reach Ray.  He tried to shove through me, but I held him there until security arrived.  You can't suspend someone for throwing a fit or even really for threatening to fight.  You also can't suspend someone for making a sex tape - the board just hasn't written that policy yet.  So, Cory got off with a two day sentence in In School Suspension for causing a major disruption.

   Cory took a day off of school to hide his embarrassment, but when he returned he was put into ISS.  Another student in ISS, Leandre (on a 2 day ISS sentence for cussing out 3 teachers in one day), spent the entire day making fun of Cory and using all of the homophobic slurs he could think of, which was a lot.  Cory took his insults the first day without saying much - he was brooding and plotting instead. Leandre also had a 2 day sentence in ISS, so Cory planned his revenge for the next day.

On Day 2 Cory arrived in In School and Leandre started up again with the insults. Just as Leandre was finishing a long series of gay jokes, a group of people entered the ISS room that the ISS monitor didn't recognize. Cory had spent all of the previous night recruiting older friends to come beat up Leandre. His girlfriend/beard Aniah coordinated the attack. She sent a text message to three of Cory's friends who were not students at LHS to come to the side door of the building. When they arrived she let them in the school and led them to the ISS room where they jumped Leandre. No one knows how Cory convinced these friends to come into the building for an attack, because they were all adults they were arrested and charged with trespassing and mob action. Aniah and Cory were also both suspended, and Aniah was put up for expulsion to an alternative school.

During the suspensions the drama over Cory's video died down. Short attention spans and plenty of other action made most students forget about it within a week. Cory never forgot. He had 5 days to get even angrier over the issue.  When he returned to LHS no one really made fun of him.  He was in my 7th hour class, and when he came back everyone just went on working like he wasn't even there.  Maybe they didn't care, or maybe they were scared random gangbangers would climb through the windows on Cory's command and jump them all.  Cory made it through the school day, but when the bell rang to end school he hustled outside to wait for Leandre.  When he saw Leandre he took matters into his own hands and attacked.  Since Leandre was bigger and had been in far more fights than Cory, he easily handled Cory's attack before the fight was broken up.  The city police arrived as Cory was reaching into his pocket, and when he was arrested they found a knife that he was planning on using on Leandre.

AFTERMATH

>-Cory was arrested and expelled.  He spent some time in JDC and a semester at an alternative school.  He eventually returned to LHS and finished his senior year in silence.
>-Aniah finished off her junior year at an alternative school but chose to drop out of school instead of returning for LHS for her senior year.

-Leandre actually graduated and works at a Meineke in town.

-Ray continued being a flamboyant tights wearing diva until he graduated.


University Tournament Brawl

    The sad thing about Midwest City is that nothing that happens at Lincoln High gets noticed.  Nothing that happens in the building gets reported in the newspaper or even really talked about around town.  People assume LHS is a rough school, but they really have no idea.  The fights that happen in the school are dealt with by the school and news of them goes no further than that.  The crimes that happen in the school go on the county commitment report, but only if the arrested student is 18 years old or older.  The only story that ever made the news was Gang Wars Day, but it only warranted a short mention in the newspaper as multiple arrests being made at LHS.  As long as problems stayed within the walls of LHS, or at least within a few blocks of the building, no one in town really cared.  That is, until our students invaded the campus of the liberal arts college in town and created a riot during a basketball tournament.

Over the Martin Luther King Day weekend our school was invited to play in a varsity basketball tournament at the college in town. There were several schools in the tournament, including Lincoln High's cross town rival Jefferson High School. Lincoln High vs. Jefferson High games always draw massive crowds, and the college basketball stadium was much larger than a high school gym, so the crowd that weekend was even larger. Our students were in full attendance, as were Jefferson's students. Jefferson is small version of Lincoln High, with the same student demographics and the same problems. Combining the two populations into one building with no teachers was a recipe for disaster.

Brenae was senior who usually stayed out of trouble, but thought she was one of the toughest girls in school. She was about 5'10" 200 pounds and played middle for the school volleyball team. She had never been in a fight at school, but the MLK tournament was her perfect opportunity to make her fighting debut. A group of girls from Jefferson had been talking trash about Lincoln High on Twitter leading up the game, so Brenae and her friends replied and started up a full-fledged Twitter war. Apparently to a high school student in Midwest City this is serious business, so groups of girls from both schools began circling the stadium giving each other angry stare downs.

When you go to a school where fights are a norm, stare downs can pretty easily escalate into shouting matches, which can escalate even more easily into fights. Brenae wasted no time in gathering a massive crew of male and female LHS students and brought them down to the lobby to intimidate a group of Jefferson kids. JHS kids think the same way that LHS kids do, so they brought a huge crowd. The university in Midwest City is not that large, but they do have a campus police force. Lincoln High and Jefferson High also had some campus security guards present, and a few administrators. The students must've thought they could act the same way they do at school in public with no consequences. A girl from Jefferson walked up to Brenae and started screaming in her face. Brenae took a swing and all hell broke loose. More than twenty-five students from each school began brawling in the lobby while a few cops could only stand and watch. Girls were piling on to each other in a huge royal rumble while the boys squared off in one on one matches round the edge of the fray.

The university police called the city for backup, but several minutes passed before they had enough adults to stop the students. One assistant principal tried to jump in and stop the fight but ended up hurting his knee as he was pushed to the ground. Finally, the police arrived in force and started throwing every student anywhere near the brawl down onto the floor. Dozens of arrests were made that night, and Lincoln High lost the basketball game to top it off. It was the perfect way for our students to celebrate MLK's message of non-violence by turning a Twitter beef into a royal rumble in a public venue.

AFTERMATH

>-Brenae and her friends were all suspended the same as if their fights had occurred in school.

>-The newspaper and local news stations all reported the brawl as a major incident involving both schools. The public took interest and pressure was put on the school board and superintendent to do something about the violence.

>-Because almost all of the students involved were juniors and seniors, it was decided that they would all forfeit their ability to go to

prom. Prom ended up being a total failure, with only about sixty students in attendance out of six hundred juniors and seniors that could have attended.

## Crime

Progressive education reformers often complain about the "school to prison pipeline" that supposedly exists in urban schools. It is true that students have been taken directly from Lincoln High to jail, but it really only happens when our school discipline system doesn't have a way to deal with the crimes being committed. A simple assault in the streets of Midwest City could lead to an arrest, but a fight in school will never result in an arrest unless another more serious crime occurs during the fight. Students have been arrested for aggravated assault, mob action, or bringing weapons into the building, but these aren't really crimes that the school can just suspend a student for to fully address. The most the school can do is suspend a student for ten days. Beyond that, the district can expel a student to an alternative school for major disruptions or repeated offenses. Once a serious crime occurs the police have to become involved or the school conditions would be worse than they already are.

Drugs and alcohol are a frequent problem at Lincoln High, but even these crimes usually don't result in arrest. Some students come to school after smoking weed daily. If they smell bad enough they are just sent home for the day after being searched. If the search turns up a small enough amount of weed to be considered for personal use they are suspended as well. The marijuana is documented and sent to the police, but they aren't arrested. Students have brought alcohol into the building with the same results. A drunken student would just be sent home. A student with alcohol on them would be suspended. Neither would be arrested. An English teacher had a student casually drinking red wine mixed with Fireball whiskey in her classroom and the only thing that happened to her was a two day suspension. A History teacher had several students in his first hour class passing cough syrup and Moscato around his room before he noticed and called security. These are technically all crimes that would probably be taken very seriously in another school, but Lincoln High can't afford to be even more of a school-to-prison pipeline than it already is, so nothing happens to them.

Weed and Chips

The only time a student can be arrested for bringing drugs to school results is when they come to school to deal. Sergio was a 19 year old special education student who was probably never going to graduate, but could legally stay in school until his 21st birthday if he wanted to. His special ed paperwork gave him free reign to do almost whatever he wanted in the building besides major crimes. State law prohibited the school from suspending him for more than 10 days in a school year without a serious crime having been committed, and even then the rules were very strict. Sergio didn't even live within the boundaries of Lincoln High, or even anywhere in the city limits of Midwest City. He lived in a completely different town, but his parents filed paperwork claiming he was homeless so he could choose to stay at Lincoln High where his customer base was located.

Sergio was always in trouble with his teachers, but he knew the rules to the special ed game and played them very well. He knew he would never be suspended for cussing at teachers or skipping class, so he did it all the time.  His assistant principal was limited to 10 days of suspension for Sergio in a year, so he wanted to make sure he could use all 10 for when Sergio did something seriously wrong.  If he used up the 10 days too early in the year Sergio could literally do whatever he wanted without being suspended.  In October of his fourth year at LHS, Sergio decided to test the limits of this rule.  He came to school with more than 10 bags of weed and started selling out of his locker.  His regulars all stopped by that morning and made their purchases.

The problem with selling weed to your friends from special ed classes is that your customers aren't going to be the smartest kids in the school.  They are going to brag all day about the weed they just bought and pretty soon that information will get to an adult.  By lunchtime word had spread to teachers that Sergio was dealing from his locker.  A school security officer walked to the 3rd floor and immediately could smell weed in the hallway, so he called for backup and an assistant principal to start the search.  In Sergio's locker they found a large purse with a family sized bag of Cheetos hot chips inside.  Beneath the hot chips there were 11 bags of weed packaged for sale.  LHS always has marijuana field test kits on hand, so it only took a few minutes to confirm that Sergio was dealing out of his locker.

The city police officer stationed in the building that day picked up Sergio from the cafeteria and brought him to the office for questioning.  Sergio denied that the weed was his, and because it was being stored in a purse, he accused his girlfriend of being the actual dealer.  The officer told him that if he wanted to blame it on his girlfriend he could, but that would just mean they were both getting arrested.  Sergio and his girlfriend had a 2 year old baby at home, and the officer let Sergio know that if they went ahead with the arrests that the baby would also be taken to Child Protective Services.  Logic was not Sergio's greatest mental ability, so he said he didn't care and that they could go ahead and arrest her for it.  Not wanting to get CPS involved in the taking of a baby, the police brought Sergio's girlfriend down separately and determined that she had no idea what was going on, so Sergio was arrested alone.

Sergio's assistant principal was so sure that this would be the end of Sergio that he used all of Sergio's remaining suspension days.  Sergio was booked by the city police and given a court date before he was bonded out by his mom.  He had eight days of suspension, but he was actually allowed back into the building after it ended.  The district office refused to expel him for fear that they would face a lawsuit for expelling a special education student.  Sergio returned to school after eight days off with free reign to do anything - the school had no more days to give him.

AFTERMATH

-Sergio's girlfriend stayed with him, she couldn't resist his charm.

-Sergio attended school for three days after his suspension ended.  The next weekend he broke into a house in Midwest City with a gun and stole a television from the residents after pointing the gun at them.  The people he robbed were able to identify him, and the police already were very familiar with him, so it was an open and shut case.  Sergio never returned to Lincoln High.

-Later in that school year another special ed student, Dontarius, brought 16 bags of weed to school in a Pringles can.  His imitation of Sergio's weed hidden inside chips trick had the same results.  The smell of chips wasn't enough to mask the massive amount of weed, so he tried to run from the police in the Commons. They stopped him with a sweep of the legs and a tackle.

Trespassing

Trespassing isn't really a major crime, but it happens so often at Lincoln High that it warrants its own section. Cory and his girlfriend Aniah allowed trespassers into the building to jump another student, and another group of trespassers came in just to watch a fight. Most trespassers are in their early 20s and are former students that never graduated. Why these adults have nothing better to do than return to the school they never even graduated from to watch or participate in a fight is beyond my comprehension, but it happens all the time. One week we had three 19 year olds come into the building during a passing period just to record video of themselves walking the halls and then they left, confusing everyone who saw them. Lamont, a former special ed student who dropped out after four years at LHS, came back the next year in the middle of a random day and just strolled through the cafeteria like he was supposed to be there. When he was stopped by security he said he was just passing through.  Another student, DeeDee, was dropped from the school rosters for skipping school more than 20 times, but showed up one random day during lunch and tried to eat with her friends.  It's not hard to spot a trespasser even in a building of 1500, so most of them are sent out pretty quickly, but it still manages to throw off everyone who sees them because of how strange it is.

The worst instances of trespassing involve adults from the city trying to find and fight students from our school.  Lance was a monster of a football player.  He was a defensive end at 6'6" 250lbs who had been recruited to play for a Division 1 university the next fall.  In the spring he was off from sports, so he spent most days after school hanging out in the Commons for fifteen to twenty minutes with his friends before heading home.

The previous night a Twitter war had erupted between a group of football players that called themselves the "Mob Team" and a group of early 20s guys, some of whom had graduated from LHS.  The outsiders claimed gang affiliation, and were not impressed that the "Mob Team" was pretending to be a gang just like them.  The Twitter war led to threats and a major street fight was scheduled. Lance didn't really consider himself a member of the Mob Team, but he was a member of the football team so he knew them all. He posted on Twitter that night to tell everyone to stop arguing and shut up about their fake gangs, but this just made him a target.

The next day at school was as normal as any other. A few high students were sent home in the morning, about twenty-five students were kicked out of class, a short lunchroom fight pumped up the cafeteria crowd, but when the final bell rang most of the adults felt like the day was pretty normal, nothing really crazy or atypical happened. Five minutes after the bell rang the routine was shattered. To trespass into a school at most times you need an insider to open the doors for you. All doors are locked at all times, and anyone who lets someone in a side door gets an automatic suspension. This deters most day-time trespassers. But when the final bell rings, the traffic coming out of the building makes it easy to slip through the doors. Three 20 year old men took their opportunity during dismissal that day.

The Twitter Warriors came through a side door near the bus line that they knew was heavily trafficked from their days at LHS. They made it down a first floor hallway heading towards the Commons before an adult recognized them.  Security was called, but most officers are stationed outside during dismissal, so they were a couple of minutes away.  The three trespassers walked up to the Mob Team and went straight for Lance - the biggest student in the crowd.  A nearby PE teacher saw the altercation beginning, but he knew that there would be no way he could stop them alone so he had to stand and watch.  The first trespasser approached Lance and threw a punch upwards at Lance's face.  Lance reached down for the intruder's hips and threw him on the ground.  He took wild swings at the other two intruders and connected, and then the Mob Team students grabbed them.  Lance returned his focus to the first intruder he had thrown to the floor.  He brought his fist back behind his head and started raining punches down on the trespasser.  Before security arrived he connected 10 haymaker punches to the face of the wannabe gangster - putting an end to any Twitter beef from the previous night.

AFTERMATH

>-Lance and his friends all scattered when the police arrived, but the police didn't give chase.

-The intruders were arrested for trespassing and mob action. They bonded out of jail and stopped bothering high school students on Twitter.

-Lance came back to school the next day and received a light suspension of one day for involvement in Twitter drama and the self-defense beat down.

-The Mob Team was investigated by the city police. They were all brought in for questioning and the police put the fear of arrest into them. They all changed their Twitter names and stopped calling themselves the "Mob Team" after the police told them the next fight would have them all labeled as gang members in the police computers.

-Trespassing became rare after this incident. Security measures increased and the punishments for letting people in became harsher. Instead of trespassing, many would be intruders chose to wait outside for the students they wanted to fight. This has happened several times but it usually results in an even quicker arrest.

Weapons

A majority of the fights at Lincoln High are one on one fights with no weapons. They start and end quickly and are broken up by staff easily. In a neighborhood like the one Lincoln High is located in, weapons are always a threat, but they don't make it into the school very often. The last time a gun was brought into a high school in Midwest City was in 2008. A special ed student pulled a revolver at Washington High School and fired six shots into a wall. Lincoln High has never had an incident involving a gun. Instead, our students get creative with their weaponry:

-Jamya brought a wrench to school and used it in a fight in the   Commons.

-Deja brought a short chain with 6 padlocks on the end and claimed it was for "self-defense."

-Kelsey brought 5 cans of soup in her purse and started throwing them at another girl in the hallway before a fight.

-Mercedes was taken to the officer for screaming at a girl like she was going to fight. When her assistant principal confronted her in the office she opened her backpack, pulled out a brick, and threatened to beat the assistant principal's head in with it.

Medieval Fight Club

Isaiah was a troubled child with a history of mental instability. He started a recruitment campaign for a Medieval Fight Club that he was trying to start outside of school. He put posters all around the building, but wasn't getting any interest. One day he decided the reason no one was interested was because they didn't know what a medieval fight club was. He planned to remedy this by bringing a replica sword to school to show everyone. He showed up one morning with a full size broadsword at the student entrance. It didn't have a sharpened edge, but it could still be used as a baseball bat style weapon, so security told him to hand it over. Isaiah was the kind of kid who sprinted to class instead of walking, so he just took off on the security officers. He ran and hid in the 4th floor loft where there were only two classrooms and he wouldn't easily be found.

About 20 minutes later he made his way back down to the Commons without his sword. Security surrounded him and started to question him about the location of the sword. Because they knew he was a flight risk, one of the officers grabbed Isaiah by the wrist to hold him in place. The officer didn't know that while Isaiah was hiding on the 4th floor he had been cutting his wrist with a razor he also had on him.  The officer pulled away his hand and found it dripping with blood.  Isaiah took off running again during the moment of confusion and disgust.  He wasn't a danger to other students, but the city police and an ambulance were called to find him and take him away.  Isaiah was found again, handcuffed to a stretcher, and carted away to the mental health department of the hospital in town.

The Pink Taser

While most of our students don't seem to have access to guns, for some reason a lot of girls have personal self-defense tasers that they keep in their purses.  I guess they know that fights are constantly happening in Midwest City and at Lincoln High so they need to be ready.

Avione was a junior who thought of himself as a playboy.  He always had different girlfriends as a freshman and sophomore and didn't think it was a big deal to cheat on them with other girls at school.  He apparently never noticed that the girls at Lincoln High were notorious for starting up huge drama and brawled with each other constantly.  Either way he didn't care, so he continued doing what he had always done.  Early junior year he started dating Amiya, and they actually made it almost through most of that school year as a couple.  Late in their junior year however, rumors started to fly as they always do at LHS.  Another junior girl Jailynn had just given birth to a baby daughter and had recently returned to school.  Jailynn was always quiet about who the father was, but eventually word got out that Avione was the father.  It didn't matter if the math didn't add up exactly right, Amiya was furious.  Instead of getting mad at Avione though, she targeted Jailynn.

Amiya and Jailynn were both in my 8th hour class.  They didn't sit near each other and I never saw them speak, so I never knew there was an issue between them.  One day our 8th hour was released early for a pep assembly in the gym, so I released my students and then followed them to the gym.  On the way down, Amiya approached Jailynn and started screaming at her.  She accused Jailynn of trying to steal Avione and before any reply was given she started swinging.  Jailynn grabbed Amiya's hair and they both locked on to each other.  While holding Jailynn's hair with one hand, Amiya reached into her pocket with the other and pulled out a small pink women's self-defense taser.  Before she could use it I grabbed Jailynn and pulled her away hard enough to rip out hair from both girls.  Security guards tackled Amiya to the floor because they saw the taser as well.  Amiya was cuffed and arrested for bringing weapons into the school, and Jailynn was taken to the office and suspended for fighting.

AFTERMATH

-Avione and Amiya sadly broke up.

-Avione and Jailynn got back together and stayed at Lincoln High for a couple of weeks.  Students made fun of them constantly and so they both decided to move to Jailynn's sister's house out of state.  Jailynn had been staying with a sister in Midwest City and Avione had been staying with his grandma, so the move wasn't out of the ordinary for either of them.

-Amiya continued at Lincoln High and was pregnant within 6 months by her new boyfriend Deandre.

-Avione actually transferred back to LHS late in his senior year after things with Jailynn didn't work out.  He graduated after lying low for a few months.

The Prize Fighter

Amiya was not the only girl to bring a weapon to school to settle a feud. Laquasha was another junior girl with a history of violence. She had been in a few fights at school as a freshman and sophomore and probably many more on the streets. She had a problem with another junior girl named Teresa but could never really explain why. In March of her junior year she decided she would end their problems by beating up Teresa at school. She showed up one morning with Vaseline covering her face to deflect punches like she was a professional boxer. When security saw her come in they pulled her aside and asked Laquasha Ali what she was doing. She didn't try to hide it - she just told them that she was here to fight. They took her up to her assistant principal to try to hold an intervention meeting with her before the fight happened. At the meeting Laquasha calmly explained that no matter what, the next time she saw Teresa they would fight. Her assistant principal adviser her to settle it outside of school or face suspension and then sent her home for the day.

Laquasha must not have seen Teresa that night, because she returned to school the next day ready to fight again. She left her Vaseline at home to make it less obvious to the student entrance security, but as soon as she arrived she headed to wait outside of Teresa's 1st hour class.

Teresa knew about the possibility of a fight so she came to school that day with a plan to get escorted to all of her classes by her friend Kayla. She also brought a spray can of mace in her purse just in case things got out of hand. Her 1st hour class was up in a quiet part of the building - the 2$^{nd}$ floor science hallway. The 2nd floor science hall had only four classrooms all taught by older teachers who were very unlikely to intervene in a fight. Security spent every morning in the Commons and at the student entrance, so they were nowhere near the area. As soon as Teresa reached the top of the stairs Laquasha pulled a string out of her pocket with a padlock tied to the end. She started spinning the lock around over her head and walking towards Teresa. Teresa immediately pulled out her mace and started spraying it at Laquasha. Once they were close enough they started throwing punches. Teresa got inside the padlock lasso and avoided getting hit in the face with it. Kayla jumped in as well and started hitting Laquasha in her ribs. Teresa kept her finger on the trigger of the mace for the entire fight and turned the entire science hall into a cloud of teargas.

When security arrived the hallway was already filled with mace, but when they saw the weapons that the girls had they all pulled out their own police-grade mace and fired at the girls. All three girls were too crazed to go down. They fought with their eyes closed instead of falling to the floor, so security had to jump in. It took five adults to separate the three girls, and they were all arrested for fighting with weapons at school.

AFTERMATH

> -Laquasha was given a maximum length suspension and put up for expulsion. She did not return to LHS.
> -Teresa and Kayla both returned after six day suspensions and eventually graduated.

Violence Against Staff

Students are free to beat each other up and the only consequence most of them face is a five day break from school. Fights are usually broken up by school security guards who are armed with mace and handcuffs. They only use handcuffs if a student is resisting them and they only use mace if a student has a weapon.  Teachers are not required to or even expected to break up fights, but many of them do.  There is always a risk of getting injured when stepping into a fight, and almost all of the injuries that happen result in no additional punishments to the students fighting.  I have been punched while breaking up two different fights.  I have also been pushed by a girl after I broke up her fight.  The definition of "assault on a staff member" is not clear cut.  If a teacher gets punched in a fight because they got in between two students punching each other, the students are not technically or legally assaulting the teacher.  The teacher is just in the way.  If a security guard throws out their back while trying to drag a student away, then they shouldn't have been dragging so hard.  The student wouldn't be liable for that either.  The only time a student can be arrested for assault against a staff member is if they deliberately turn to face the staff member and continue swinging with intent to hit the staff member.  In that case the student would be arrested and charged with aggravated assault.  All of these examples have happened at Lincoln High, but there are two examples that were obvious instances of assault on staff members.

Noah vs. Mr. McGee

Mr. McGee was a veteran math teacher who had good rapport with his students. His class was difficult but most students liked taking it because he taught it. Higher level students got his sense of humor and were willing to work hard for him. Being such a long time teacher though, he was a little old-school and traditional when it came to discipline. He was quick to eject students who didn't get serious in his class and a lot of the students with behavior issues hated his class. He had a student, Noah, who he constantly needed to remove from class for his behavior.

Noah began class one day in October by arguing with the student next to him. Tyrell was tired of Noah disrupting class and getting kicked out, so he told him to shut up. Noah stood up and started heading towards Tyrell, who stood up. Mr. McGee stepped between the two and told them to stop. Noah pushed Tyrell so Mr. McGee grabbed Noah's arms. Noah turned to Mr. McGee and broke from his grasp. He brought his hands up to Mr. McGee's throat and started to choke him out. He held his grip for a few seconds before several students intervened and dragged Noah into the hallway.  Security arrived shortly and arrested Noah.

After a student hits a teacher the teacher is always given the option to press charges.  Even in a case where it is clear that the teacher was just in between punches being thrown they always have the option, though they are told the charges will always be dropped.  Mr. McGee chose to press charges because Noah wasn't accidently choking the wrong guy, he deliberately attacked Mr. McGee.  Noah was arrested and had a short trial where he admitted what he did and was sentenced.

AFTERMATH

> -Noah spent a short time in JDC and was then transferred to a district alternative school.  A year later he returned to Lincoln High even though Mr. McGee was still an employee.  He was never scheduled for another math class with Mr. McGee.

Virginia vs. Mrs. Roberts

Mrs. Roberts had been teaching at Lincoln High for over 10 years in the self-contained behavior and emotional disability special ed class.  She was great with these students and was used to defusing most situations that occurred in her room. Fights happened a lot in her classroom, but she always had a large former basketball player that worked as an aide in her room, so there wasn't much danger to her. Mr. Thomas would step in and stop most fights before they started and then security would remove the disrupting students. Mr. Thomas had a major limp from an old knee injury and scheduled a surgery for late in the school year to give himself the entire summer to recover. This meant that for a couple of months Mrs. Roberts would have a different aide in her room and would have to step in more often to intervene in fights.

Like many of Mrs. Roberts's students, Virginia was emotionally unstable. She was medicated to control her emotions, but they didn't always work because she didn't always take them. During Mr. Thomas' absence Virginia became angry with a boy in her class. Throughout the day her anger built up and eventually she lashed out in rage. She attacked Darren with such ferocity that Mrs. Roberts and her substitute aide didn't have time to stop her. Mrs. Roberts tried to grab Virginia from behind, but Virginia turned around and slammed Mrs. Roberts into the wall. She then turned back to Darren and continued attacking him. The aide ran to the hallway to find help, so Mrs. Roberts stepped in again. Virginia grabbed Mrs. Roberts and brought her to the ground and started wrestling with her on the floor. She wasn't throwing punches; she was just trying to get on top of Mrs. Roberts while Mrs. Roberts was trying to get on top of her. The aide returned with another teacher who dragged Virginia to her feet. Security then arrived and returned calm to the room. Mrs. Roberts was in the hallway with Virginia while security was talking with Darren. Virginia decided she wasn't done, so she started cussing at Darren from the doorway. Mrs. Roberts grabbed Virginia by the wrist, so Virginia turned around and punched Mrs. Roberts in the face. Both security guards tackled Virginia and handcuffed her on the floor.

Even though Virginia was a special ed student, she could have been expelled for assaulting a teacher. Mrs. Roberts was required to write a statement explaining what happened during the incident so the district had the evidence it needed to process a special education expulsion. In her report Mrs. Roberts wrote that Virginia hit her during the course of a fight that she was trying to break up. She failed to mention that Virginia turned on her three separate times and intentionally attacked her, so the district would not expel Virginia. They claimed to need more evidence, but would not allow Mrs. Roberts to amend her statement.

AFTERMATH

>  -Virginia served a standard fighting suspension and was also arrested for assault, but was not expelled from school. She eventually was able to return to LHS and was put back into Mrs. Roberts's class, as Mrs. Roberts was the only teacher that taught students like Virginia.

Theft

Violent crimes and drug crimes are daily problems at Lincoln High. Fights create the most drama at school and involve the most students and drugs get the most police attention, but theft is another frequent crime that is the most difficult to solve. Student phones are constantly being stolen at Lincoln High. Most phones that disappear are never seen again. A thief can take a stolen phone to a store at the mall in town and be given cash with no questions asked. Within a day all evidence of most thefts are gone.  A phone stolen from a player's locker during a volleyball game ended up with a criminal in St. Louis who was arrested with it on unrelated charges the next day.  The girl in that case got lucky, but most kids will never see their stolen phones again.


Mr. Valenti's iPhone

   Mr. Valenti was a student teacher from a university about an hour away from Lincoln High.  He was a very small guy (5'7" 130lbs) from the suburbs of a nearby city.  He was student teaching sophomore World History and senior Government classes in the Social Studies department for Mrs. Brown.  Mr. Valenti thought of himself as a crusader who could come in from the rich suburbs and help save the poor students of Lincoln High.  He proved his naivety by leaving his cell phone on his desk every hour as he was teaching.

   Victor was from a large family where most of the men had criminal records.  His dad and older brother were in prison for gang activity and another brother was at an alternative school for mob action fighting at school.  Victor embraced his family traditions, so when he saw Mr. Valenti's iPhone sitting unguarded on a desk, he swiped it.  Mr. Valenti noticed it was missing and called security, but there wasn't much they could do.  Security individually searched each student in the class but couldn't find the phone.  Victor had hidden it inside a pocket of the shorts he was wearing under his jeans.  Hundreds of cell phones have been stolen at LHS, many from teachers.  There isn't much security can do unless someone talks, and no one in Mr. Valenti's class was talking.

There was one last option for Mr. Valenti.  His phone had a GPS tracking app called Find My iPhone that could locate his phone within a few hundred feet.  The app was useless inside the building because it was too crowded, so Mr. Valenti waited until after the final bell rang to start tracking his phone.  He got in his car with another student teacher and waited for students groups to break apart.  He saw his phone was moving slowly through one of the neighborhoods near the school, so he followed it.  When he arrived at the blip on his GPS, he saw a group of 8 boys walking home.  Victor and his like-minded friends were walking together through their neighborhood - a neighborhood known for its high crime rate.  This didn't really bother the boys, because they were part of the reason for the crime rate spike. They had been in street fights, robbed houses, and vandalized cars parked on the street. Mr. Valenti, a suburbanite, had no idea what he was getting into.

Mr. Valenti stepped out of his car and approached the boys. He only knew Victor, so he knew that Victor must have his phone. He didn't bother to call the police; he just figured he would handle it on his own. He walked into the middle of the group and demanded his cell phone back. The boys closed ranks around Mr. Valenti and asked what cell phone he was talking about. Mr. Valenti explained that he had tracked them on GPS so he knew they had it. After cussing him out they ask him why they shouldn't just beat him up and take his wallet. At this point Mr. Valenti was a little nervous. He started to realize he really didn't have any clue where he was. The neighborhoods in Midwest City were a huge grid with the only real landmarks being the major streets. They weren't anywhere near a major street. Maybe Mr. Valenti convinced them not to beat up a teacher, or maybe the boys decided a daylight attack wouldn't go unnoticed, so Victor admitted that he had the phone. He told Mr. Valenti that he wouldn't just give it back, but he would sell it back to him. Realizing that he was in over his head, Mr. Valenti gave Victor $20 for his own phone.

AFTERMATH

>-Mr. Valenti lived to tell his story, but he didn't officially report it to anyone, so there were no charges filed for theft.
>-Victor continued as a student at LHS until he and his friends got involved in a murder outside of school. He was never seen again at Lincoln High.

GTA: Teacher Lot

Mrs. Wade was a counselor at Lincoln High. Her main job was meeting with and counseling students with emotional problems that attended LHS. This took the bulk of her time, but she was also responsible for registering and scheduling one fourth of the students into their classes.

Lincoln High has a high student mobility rate. Students drop from school weekly without any notice given to the school. Counselors have to keep track of who hasn't been at school in a while and make calls to see if they have dropped. They also have to handle students who come in every week to register for school. Some students register late in a year because they have just moved to Midwest City.  Others register late because they were just hanging around the house and their parents took a few weeks to get them to school.  The final group of late registration students are transfers from alternative schools.

Deangelo was a transfer student from an alternative school - the Midwest County Juvenile Detention Center.  Deangelo had just served a sentence for robbery and was being released directly back into the public school system.  There is no step-down school from prison to Lincoln High.  As soon as a student finishes a sentence, they are sent right back into the schools.  The district has a few alternative school options, but they are only for expelled students who have gone through a paperwork process with the district.  Because of this, direct from prison transfers are common at LHS.

In January Deangelo was released from JDC and was required to register at Lincoln High as a condition of his probation.  He was entering as a junior and was assigned Mrs. Wade as his counselor.  He entered his office with his required paperwork for registration and Mrs. Wade walked him through the process.  He would be taking English 3, US History, Anatomy, and Transitions Math, along with some electives.  Once they agreed on a schedule, Mrs. Wade left her office to make copies of Deangelo's paperwork and to print him a schedule.  She left Deangelo in her office as she had done with hundreds of her other students.

Mrs. Wade was pregnant, and even she admitted that small things had been slipping her mind recently.  That morning she had forgotten to lock her purse in her desk, and had left her keys next to her keyboard.  Deangelo saw the keys and took his opportunity.  As soon as Mrs. Wade left to make copies he grabbed her keys and took off out a side door of the counseling center. He went straight to the staff parking lot and started clicking the lock button on her key fob.  This led him straight to her car, which he stole immediately.

When Mrs. Wade returned to her office she thought it was strange that Deangelo was missing.  It took her about 10 minutes to notice that her keys were also missing.  She saw an assistant principal in the hallway and they both walked to the teacher parking lot to see if her car was still there.  They couldn't find it so they immediately called the police.

In most cases it would be difficult for the police to quickly find a stolen silver Buick.  There was nothing remarkable about Mrs. Wade's car that would make it easily noticeable as stolen.  Deangelo probably thought he was pretty slick; he had gotten away with his crime easily.  He must have forgotten that he had just handed Mrs. Wade his registration paperwork which contained his name, his mom's name, his phone number, and his address.  It didn't take a veteran detective to solve the case of the stolen car.  Police just went to Deangelo's house and waited for him.  He rounded the corner and was immediately stopped and arrested.  Mrs. Wade's car had to be processed, but she had it back before the end of the school day.

AFTERMATH

> -Mrs. Wade started making sure she locked up her purse and keys first thing every morning.
>
> -Deangelo was sent back to JDC where there are no cars to easily steal.

Exposure

The last major crime that affects our school is impossible to quantify and almost never gets reported to the police.  No arrests have ever been made for what the students call "getting exposed," or what adults would refer to as child pornography.

We don't really know what compels girls to send naked pictures of themselves to boys at school. This is a fairly new phenomenon that is made easy by smart phones and apps like Snapchat that supposedly delete pictures after a few seconds. It seems like common sense that a high school boy who gets a naked picture of a girl from school will show his friends, but a lot of girls at Lincoln High don't seem to care.

The story is always the same. A girl sends a picture of herself to a boy. The boy keeps it a secret for a while, but eventually lets it slip to his friends. His friends peer pressure him into showing the picture, or they just steal it off of his phone. Once the confidentiality is broken between the girl and the original boy, the picture spreads easily. There isn't an adult in the building who would willingly search a student's phone for nude pictures of other students, so the teachers have no knowledge of any of this process.

Because drama is entertaining to a lot of LHS students, every few months random groups of boys organize "exposure" events on Facebook. Students encourage each other to post all of the naked pictures that they have collected on their cell phones to the internet for everyone to see. Girls get "exposed" when someone posts their picture to the internet.

The day after an exposure event is when the adults notice the drama. Not many girls know how to handle their emotions after they've been exposed. Some probably say nothing and just take a few days off of school, but others come to school ready to fight anyone who talks to them about it. The problem is knowing who to fight. The girl has to decide between fighting the boy she originally sent the picture to, the person who exposed her, the person who organized the exposure event, the people who made fun of her in the comments section of the photo, or just the first person who looks at her funny that morning.

Patience chose to fight the person who exposed her. In her case a girl had gotten ahold of a picture of her and posted it online, so that made her decision easier. The next day after being exposed she came to school for the sole purpose of fighting. She jumped Aaliyah, got a few solid hits in, and then took her five day suspension. When she came back the students had moved on to the next drama and there were no more problems.

Rachelle chose to fight the first person who said something to her about it. She made it all the way to lunch before someone made fun of her, so she started swinging immediately. Afterwards she didn't really care that her photo was out there, she just said she didn't want to hear anyone talking about it at school.

This has happened so many times at Lincoln High with the exact same results. Almost every girl decided to take matters into their own hands instead of getting their parents, school administration, or the police involved. Maybe they are too embarrassed or think they can just fight to solve any problem. The national news reports stories like this all the time from other schools around the country, but Lincoln High kids just deal with it on their own.

**PARENTS**

To understand what makes a Lincoln High student you have to look at a few sources. Lincoln High students come from a community that acts very similar to the way they act at school. They go to primary and middle schools that have the same behavior issues, with teachers at all levels using questionable methods. Our students spend 7 hours of 180 days per year in our schools. The rest of their time is spent either in the community or with their parents. We as teachers don't get to witness the parenting that takes place at home, but sometimes we do get to witness parenting that takes place at school.

A large group of Lincoln High parents have the mindset that a high school age student doesn't really need parental contact or involvement at school. This could actually be true for a lot of our students. A teacher probably won't try to make contact with a parent of an A or B student. One of the problems at Lincoln High is that it's almost impossible to contact a majority of parents, even those who we need to contact because of serious issues at school. 90% of parents don't list an email with the school and around half of the phone numbers listed with the school don't work. If I tried to call my students' parents I might get lucky and get a real person, but most of the time I'd run into a full voicemail, a nonexistent voicemail, or a disconnected phone number. The school has parent-teacher conferences twice a year. At my last conference I had 20 parents out of 150 students, and every single one of them was the parent of a student in my UP class, only a few of whom I really needed to talk to.

This could explain why a lot of students at Lincoln High don't seem to care very much about school, but it doesn't really explain why there is so much violence in the building. Once you see Lincoln High parents in action though it becomes pretty obvious where all the fights come from. LHS parents commonly use corporal punishment to discipline their children. This is a hotly debated topic in some communities, but not Midwest City. An English teacher had a parent stop by the classroom to pull out her son Tavias. Tavias had been screwing around in class and not taking anything seriously, so his mom came into the building, pulled him out of English class, and smacked him in the head right in front of the door to the classroom. Hitting your kids is just what you do in Midwest City to teach them a lesson.

Chandler's Dad

Chandler was a sophomore who was failing all of his classes. He would be at school every day, but really just came to socialize. He would skip a lot of classes, and when he attended he would find himself kicked out more often than not. Chandler's main past-time was cussing at teachers. He would come in a room and immediately call his teacher a "lookin' ass" or some other nonsense insult. After repeating this trend for weeks, Chandler was finally called down to his assistant principal for a suspension.

Mr. Kohler, an assistant principal, called Chandler down to his office for a meeting. When a student is suspended a parent is also called and asked to pick up their child. Chandler's dad was enraged that he had to leave work to pick up his misbehaving son from school. Mr. Chandler made it through the meeting with Mr. Kohler, but he couldn't hold in his anger before he left the building. As soon as they left Mr. Kohler's office Chandler's dad shoved his son. He pushed him into the lockers and started screaming at him. Chandler just laughed at this as most teenagers would, so his dad punched him in the face. Mr. Kohler didn't really know what to do, so he just watched as Chandler and his dad got into a full-fledged fight in the hallway. Chandler took his dad and hip tossed him to the floor, and they both wrestled there until Mr. Kohler decided to have security escort them both out.

Selena's Step-Mom

Step parents are more common at Lincoln High than they are at most schools. It's something the students are used to, but not all teenagers respect their step parents, and Selena was no exception to this. She thought her step-mom had no right to try to parent her, and she would let her know this constantly. Selena was a junior who was doing pretty well at school. She was a player on the volleyball and track teams, and had pretty good grades. She had been in a few fights as a younger student, but seemed to have turned her act around.

Despite turning around her behavior at school, Selena had not changed at home. Her step-mom was constantly arguing with her and telling her what to do. Selena didn't respect her, so she would argue back. Her dad mostly stayed out of it, so one night Selena's step-mom kicked her out of the house. Selena had to stay at a friend's house for a few nights. One evening she returned to her house to get some clothes, and her step-mom confronted her. The confrontation escalated into a fight, which Selena won, and the police arrived. Selena ended up moving to Memphis to live with her mom and was unable to finish out her school career at LHS.

Chandrea's Mom

Parents using corporal punishment on their own children may or may not be right, but it is a nationwide issue that doesn't really set Midwest City apart from anywhere else. Our examples of spankings turning into fights could happen anywhere else, but there are a few parents in Midwest City that set our town apart from the rest.

Chandrea was a senior who had just returned to school from maternity leave. She was trying to focus on school so she could graduate on time, but one day in March she got caught up in the unavoidable drama of Jasmine. Jasmine and her friend Alyssa had been trash talking Chandrea on Twitter and Facebook for a while, and Chandrea had been doing a good job of ignoring it. The two troublemakers were making fun of Chandrea for having a kid while in high school. She didn't really care as long as the insults didn't distract her from school. Jasmine was not one to give up easily when her drama didn't spill over into the school.  She and Alyssa approached Chandrea at her locker and began talking trash to her face.  Despite being outnumbered, Chandrea rose to the challenge and slapped Jasmine in the face.  The three girls began a slap-fest that resulted in a few bleeding scratches and a pile of weave littering the floor.

   The three girls did not let a suspension from school stop their drama.  The weekend came and both girls gathered a larger group of supporters.  The groups agreed to meet at Chandrea's house to settle the issue.  Jasmine and Alyssa showed up with a couple of friends and came on to Chandrea's porch.  Chandrea came out of her house with two friends.  The girls argued loudly for a few minutes when Chandrea's mom came out of the house with a baseball bat.  That's when the fight started again.  All of the girls attacked each other and Chandrea's mom jumped right into the fray.  She didn't get any major league swings, but she did hit Jasmine a few times in the side with the bat.  The fight was broken up by neighbors and no police were called.  The school usually hears about major neighborhood fights like this, but Chandrea's assistant principal learned about the brawl too late to change what happened next.

The following Tuesday all three girls returned from their suspension. None of them shared a class, so the morning was actually peaceful. By lunch time school officials heard about the neighborhood fight and decided to investigate. They called in Chandrea's mom, and she wasted no time in driving up to the school. When she arrived she entered the office as all visitors do, but she entered in a rage. She started screaming at the front desk secretary to find her daughter so she could pull her out of school. The secretary asked her to wait for a principal to arrive, but Chandrea's mom was on a rampage. She stormed out of the main office screaming and started running down the hallway towards the Commons. The principal and a counselor saw her and gave chase. She made it to the entrance to the Commons before school security caught up to her. As she was being handcuffed she screamed that she was going to find and beat up Jasmine again. Chandrea and Jasmine were in the Commons at the time eating lunch, and they both ran over and started fighting for a third time. Chandrea's mom was banned from the building and both girls were suspended for a second time.

Ariel's Mom

When parents enter the building and try to fight other students it is a major security concern. There are processes in place to prevent intruders from trespassing into the building, but when the intruder is a parent it makes it much more difficult to screen and stop them from doing any hard. It becomes impossible when the parent is also an employee of the school, like Ariel's mom. Ariel's mom was a cafeteria worker at Lincoln High. Her daughter was a freshman who hadn't quite figured out how to behave in high school, and was frequently caught up in drama in the hallways and lunch room. Drama can grow exponentially sometimes, and when two students decide to fight it can cause multiple other students to fight as well, even if the issues are totally unrelated. One week Lincoln High had a fight in lunch for four straight days, and by Friday it was just expected that a fight needed to happen. Ariel and her friends fulfilled expectations.

As the bell rang to end the first lunch period students were milling around the Commons more so than usual. A large group of freshman girls had gathered in the corner and appeared to be in an animated discussion. A cafeteria worker could also be seen in the crowd.  In the middle of the circle Ariel and another girl, Faith, were in an argument.  Faith grabbed on to Ariel's hair and started hitting her.  The other girls all screamed in excitement as the two tried to slap each other down to the floor.  Typically, an adult right next to a fight would step in and try to stop it, especially if the fighters were two small freshmen girls, but the cafeteria worker in the crowd was Ariel's mom, and she was busy rooting her daughter on.

After security managed to push through the crowd and separate the two girls, Ariel's mom gave a celebratory yell across the Commons and shouted "ya'll gonna know Ariel!" several times at the remaining girls in the circle.  She was disciplined by the cafeteria manager but for some reason wasn't fired on the spot.  This sort of behavior must be seen as acceptable even among some adults in Midwest City.

Martasia's Dad

Martasia was a freshman that had problems getting to school on time.  Lincoln High had a policy that students that arrived tardy too many times to school could be dropped unless they provided legitimate documentation to excuse their tardiness.

Martasia's dad was called into the school to meet with an assistant principal about Martasia's tardy problem. When he arrived at school he became instantly angry at the possibility of his daughter being kicked out of school for being tardy. He argued that her grades were fine so it shouldn't matter if she is on time to class. The assistant principal tried to calmly explain that Martasia would not be automatically dropped, but her dad wasn't willing to listen to logic.

As he got louder and louder a school security officer happened to enter the office. Martasia's dad took this as a threat and started to close the gap between himself and the assistant principal. The AP decided that the meeting was going nowhere, so they asked him to leave the building. The security officer approached him and tried to get him to follow her out, but he wouldn't move. He began to show signs that he was ready to fight one of them, so the security officer pulled out her mace and told him he needed to leave now. He must've thought his invitation to a school meeting was an invitation to a fight, because he pulled a knife out of his pocket and flashed it in the security guards face. Luckily before it could escalate into a murder he came to his senses and ran out of the building. The police tracked him down and arrested him for aggravated assault, and Martasia was on time the next day.

Thompsons vs. Docketts

The Hatfields and the McCoys had nothing on Lincoln High's own Thompsons and Docketts. The two families started a feud that fueled two months of brawling on and off school property.

The Thompsons were a large family headed by a single mom, Tianna. Tianna had four children at Lincoln High from three different fathers. Alonzo, a junior, was the oldest. He was actually supposed to be a senior but he was kicked out of school for fighting and spent most of that time on the streets instead of attending his alternative school. Trumpet, named after his dad's favorite instrument, was a 17 year old sophomore in his second attempt at that year. He was a special education student who had also spent a year at an alternative school. Darquell, Trumpet's full brother, was a true freshman but was slightly old for his grade. Adrianna, the only girl, was a true freshman who was slightly young for her grade and was the center of the family feud.

The Dockett family was also headed by a single mom, Quandrea. Quandrea had two children at Lincoln High. Quandesha and Dae'Quan were twins in their freshman year at LHS. They also had a cousin, Tamika, who was a sophomore. Tamika's brother was in his 20s and had graduated a few years before from LHS.

Trumpet and Darquell fought people all over school and all over town. Trumpet's favorite spot was the parking lot of an abandoned grocery store halfway between the school and his house. He would meet opponents there several times per school year for boxing matches. He was a special education student, so he was difficult to suspend and almost impossible to expel. His mom knew this and made sure to bring it up any time an assistant principal tried to suspend him. All three of the Thompson boys would not hesitate to back up their sister Adrianna, even though she was clearly tough enough to handle anything on her own.

Adrianna and Quandesha were the alpha females of the freshman class. They were the toughest and loudest girls at school and both had a large flock of followers.  Adrianna was built like an athlete and had arms that no one would want to get punched by.  Quandesha was a powerhouse who could bulldoze through anyone.  It was only a matter of time before the two girls became rivals.  By November it was clear that a showdown was approaching.  Both groups started trash talking on Facebook, where Quandesha announced that the issue would be settled the next day after school.

The unstoppable force met the immovable object after school the next day in the Commons.  Huge crowds gathered for the matchup in what was predicted to be the fight of the year - the sister of the famous Trumpet versus the newcomer loudmouth freshman.  The hype was too big.  Adults learned of the fight before it could occur and a large security presence made it impossible for the two groups to meet each other.  The crowds were cleared and both girls were brought to the office for an intervention discussion.  The discussion didn't go very well.  Both girls ended up screaming at each other, and Adrianna stated matter-of-factly that she would fight Quandesha and beat her the next time they saw each other no matter what the adults said.  Both moms were called to pick up their daughters, but neither could be suspended.

The next day the 1500 students and 150 staff members at LHS all knew what was coming. Even the city police knew and sent an extra officer to the building. The girls made it through the day without running into each other, but at dismissal all hell broke loose. The Dockett mom came into the Commons at dismissal with her nephew, a 20 year old LHS graduate. They met up with Quandesha, her twin Dae'Quan, and her cousin Tamika. Adrianna was surrounded by her crew including all three brothers, but they would have to walk by the Dockett family reunion to exit the building. As the Thompson family was exiting the Dockett mom taunted them, so they all stopped and turned. Adrianna charged at Quandesha and grabbed her by the hair. Tamika jumped in to defend her cousin and made it a two on one fight. At the same time Darquell and Trumpet jumped in to take on Dae'Quan and his older cousin. Darquell squared off with Dae'Quan and Trumpet took the adult. The three fights raged on as the Dockett mom stood screaming and cheering on her children. She neared the fight between Adrianna and Quandesha and looked as if she was about to join.

Alonzo, seeing this, ran up to the Dockett mom and punched her in the side of the head. There's no such thing as a mature adult in the Dockett family, so Quandesha's mom started swinging on the high school student Alonzo.

A large group fight is always hard to sort out. There aren't enough security officers in the school to handle nine fighters, and teachers are hesitant to step in when the crowd is that large. When security arrived to break up the Dockett vs. Thompson fight, five officers grabbed the first five people they could. The girls kept trying to fight, but the boys tried to scatter. Security managed to get all of the girls to stop and got them to the office. Alonzo, who was fighting an adult, left the building undetected. Quandesha's older cousin, who should have been arrested, was grabbed by a security guard who happened to know him from outside of work. The security guard was new on the job and didn't realize that it wasn't appropriate to act friendly towards an adult that had just finished fighting a student. He walked the older cousin to the door and actually let him leave. Trumpet and Darquell noticed this so they took off after him. Out on the street in front of the school they jumped the cousin and started up the fight again. All three of them were arrested by city police. Six of the seven students who were involved were suspended that day, but Alonzo escaped suspension by sneaking out during the chaos.

The next few days were peaceful. Alonzo showed up to school for a couple of days before the assistant principals realized he should've been suspended also, but he got what was coming to him. When a large fight like this occurs, the five day suspension period can be like the eye of a hurricane. All of the students who fought were scheduled to return on the same day (except Alonzo). When they returned it was almost expected that the fighting would continue because of the bad terms that it all ended on.

Adrianna wanted a solid victory, not a split decision due to security interference. The day they all returned the fighting restarted almost immediately. The first Dockett that Adrianna saw that day was Tamika, and she wasted no time. Between 1$^{st}$ and 2$^{nd}$ hour the girls reignited the feud in a 3$^{rd}$ floor fight outside of Tamika's English class. Tamika plainly won the fight, which had to be broke up by two security guards, two teachers, and a counselor. Tamika nearly threw Adrianna off of the balcony overlooking the staircase down to the 2$^{nd}$ floor as she savagely beat her jaw and nose. Adrianna came away with blood gushing from her mouth and nose but still managed to resist the security guards. Both girls were given another round of five day suspensions, but the fighting that day was not over.

As the day was winding down, the remaining members of the Dockett family were planning another Commons showdown for dismissal. The Thompson brothers weren't too concerned about the feud, their main goal in the first brawl was to protect their sister who had already been sent home, so they didn't expect what was coming next. At dismissal Dae'Quan and Quandesha found Darquell and attacked him without warning. He didn't really have a chance to fight back as they brought him to the ground and started punching and kicking him. Security tried to intervene, but once again they resisted. Quandesha even tried to wrestle one officer as he struggled to pull her away. The Dockett twins were also given another round of suspensions, and Quandesha was put on the expulsion hearing list for her extreme behavior during the struggle with security.

After the second round of fighting most of the drama at school died down. Alonzo and Trumpet were the only two not suspended again, and they were both Thompson family members. Quandesha, the leader of the Dockett family, was on extended suspension and would not cause any more trouble. The only thing the school had to worry about was Adrianna's never-give-up attitude towards fighting. She returned from her second suspension the same day as Tamika and went back for a third and final fight against a Dockett girl. This time, Adrianna would not be denied a victory. She got the jump on Tamika in the freshmen hallway between classes and landed several square punches before the inevitable hair grabbing wrestling match began. As the fight was broken up the video evidence recorded by several students showed Adrianna as the clear victor. Her mom was called in to the school to pick her up for her third suspension in a row. Most parents would probably be either extremely angry or extremely embarrassed if their child was suspended for fighting 3 times in 3 days at school, but not Mrs. Thompson. She seemed almost proud of Adrianna and simply stated to one of the assistant principals, "She did what she had to do." Her mom believed that because Adrianna lost her first fight against Tamika that she had no choice but to redeem herself in the last fight.

Adrianna's mom lived these ideals.  A quick search of her name in the county jail records revealed that she had a record breaking 26 arrests for assault, battery, mob action, resisting arrest, and whatever other forms of violent minor crimes a person could commit.  After seeing her mom's rap sheet the Thompson/Dockett feud made perfect sense.  Even though Adrianna was a straight 'A' student she was still living under the roof of a violent person who obviously believed fighting was not just a valid problem solver, but a way of life.

Adrianna's assistant principal carefully reviewed everything that had happened before making a decision on Adrianna's future.  She had three consecutive suspensions for fighting, which could have been a slam dunk expulsion if that's what the school wanted.  Her AP also looked at Adrianna's grades, which were straight 'A's, her personality when not fighting, which was positive, and her parents, who were clearly a terrible influence.  It was decided that Adrianna could stay at LHS on the condition that she did nothing else for the rest of her freshman year.  She agreed that if she did anything wrong at all for the remainder of the year she would be automatically expelled, so she was allowed to return to school. This agreement, paired with the expulsion of Quandesha, is what stopped the feud.

AFTERMATH

-Adrianna Thompson continued at LHS as an honor roll student and two-sport athlete who stayed out of trouble the rest of her career.

-Alonzo Thompson returned from fighting the Dockett mom and managed to stay out of trouble until he graduated.

-Trumpet Thompson was finally expelled after his eighth fight in the same school year. Because of his special education status he was difficult to remove.

-Darquell Thompson continued at LHS as an occasional troublemaker, but wasn't involved in anything major again.

-Mrs. Thompson continued making regular appearances in the county commitment report.

-Quandesha Dockett was expelled for extreme resistance against security and was never seen at LHS again.

-Dae'Quan Dockett was sent to an alternative school for failing every class in his freshman year. He never graduated.

-Tamika Dockett distanced herself from her Dockett cousins and graduated on time.
-Mrs. Dockett was banned from the building under threat of an arrest for trespassing. She and her nephew were never seen again.
-The security guard who let the Dockett cousin walk was fired the next day for allowing an adult who had just attacked a student to leave the building.

Joseph's Dad

All of the parents discussed so far have either been occasionally violent or partially insane, but none of them compare to Joseph's dad, who was a terrible human being and a child abuser. The other parents covered are clearly bad parents, but at least their stories can be laughed about afterwards. Stories of mental or physical abuse by parents at Lincoln High are never funny, and are far too common. Teachers often have to report parents for things they hear from students. Sometimes students come to school with black eyes from fights with step-dads, or say that they haven't bathed in weeks. These incidents are reported and dealt with by an outside agency, and most of the students involved continue at Lincoln

High. This is a much bigger issue with grade school students, but it can still happen at the high school level.

Joseph's dad had been visited several times by the outside agency. Joseph's teachers first started to notice a problem in his junior year at LHS. His attendance became spotty and when he was present he spent most of class sleeping. Joseph was a quiet kid anyway, so this didn't really raise any red flags with most teachers. A couple of teachers finally did notice a problem when Joseph started coming to school without having bathed several days in a row. One of his teachers asked him if anything was going on and didn't get much of an answer. She was suspicious though so she called the outside agency with her concerns. Nothing came of her call, or of the subsequent calls placed by other teachers that school year.

During Joseph's senior year things started to get worse. Joseph appeared sick whenever he attended and was still sleeping and unclean. He had lost a lot of weight since his junior year as well. One day Joseph just stopped coming to school. He would never return to Lincoln High.

Late in what was his senior year Joseph was found dead at his dad's house.  His father called an ambulance after Joseph had been passed out on the couch for hours, but it was too late.  The EMTs also noticed strange things in Joseph's house that prompted them to call the police.  Joseph had marks on his wrists and ankles like he had been chained or tied, and he was clearly malnourished.  A police investigation revealed the horrible details of what had happened to Joseph.  His father kept him on a chain in the living room starving and beating him to death over the course of several months, and no one else in the family said or did anything.

Joseph's story was the extreme end of parental abuse at Lincoln High.  99% of the cases of abuse are far less than what happened to Joseph, but it stands out as the worst example of what can happen to Midwest City students.  Many are physically abused without anyone knowing, and others are physically abused without anything happening to their parents even if it is reported.  The outside agency responsible is too small to stop it all.

## COMMUNITY/NEIGHBORHOODS

The students of Lincoln High and their parents make up part of the larger Midwest City community that is plagued by the same problems as the school. A quick scroll through the county commitment report gives a glimpse into what kind of place Midwest City is. Violent crimes, mob actions, domestic batteries, drug sales, and robberies happen daily in Midwest City, with other major crimes sprinkled in.

The recent history of Midwest City is the same as the recent history of most major Midwestern cities. Once a booming industrial town that was considered an example for the rest of the country, changes in the last fifty years left Midwest City desperately clinging to its last remaining industry. The Great Migration of African-Americans from the South to the Midwest after World War 2 started a demographic shift in Midwest City. Black families moved north and started buying or renting houses in the classic old neighborhoods of the city. At the same time, the interstate highway system was developed, allowing commuters to reach the city for work without living in the city. This allowed established white families to move further from the center of Midwest City into neighborhoods on the edge of town or to the suburbs.

In the 1960s and 70s the city racial demographics began to transform, especially the older neighborhoods nearer to downtown. These neighborhoods became almost entirely black neighborhoods as white families moved away either out of racism, fear, or just for a chance to live in a bigger and newer house. These changes wouldn't have actually meant anything if industries in Midwest City hadn't started to close. Factories shut down, leaving the newly arrived black families with not enough jobs to support them. The neighborhoods in the old part of Midwest City also began to fall into a state of disrepair. As money disappeared crime increased, and old Midwest City became known as a place to avoid.

Lincoln High serves the old neighborhoods of Midwest City, so as the neighborhoods changed, so did the school. LHS became known as a dangerous school because of the dangerous neighborhood that it is located in. It's not uncommon to drive up to work in the morning and see people sitting on their porches drinking before 7am. There are two known crack houses right behind Lincoln High that the police have raided several times. One morning two neighborhood residents started shooting at each other at 7:45am right as busses were dropping off students, prompting a short lockdown of the school.

School Related Crime

Crime is rampant in the neighborhood around LHS, and students are often involved. Several LHS students have criminal records, though most are sealed due to the fact that they are juveniles. That doesn't mean they don't share their criminal antics with their teachers. Most arrests are for fighting or drug use, but some students go above and beyond. Malik was a student of mine who spent four years in Juvenile Detention for stealing cars when he was 12. Kenten was another student who spent time in jail for pulling a gun on someone after a fight.


Craiglist Attacks

Jermaine and Jaden were brothers and students at Lincoln High who thought of themselves as entrepreneurs. They would steal phones from other students at school and then sell them for a profit. Their business was going well but it had risks. Cameras were all over the halls at LHS so they could easily be caught. Jermaine and Jaden began brainstorming ways to expand their business.

Craiglist's Midwest City page was a popular place for people in town to buy and sell used items of questionable quality. Jermaine and Jaden decided to take their stolen phone business to Craigslist instead of selling them for a fraction of the value at a used phone store in Midwest City. Because this allowed them to remove the middle man and directly reach their customers, they were able to increase profits.

Eventually the two boys realized that they didn't have to sell stolen phones at all. They decided to instead set up meetings with people around town and simply jump then and steal their money. It was the perfect business model. They placed ads for used smart phones all over Craigslist and waiting for the replies to roll in. They set up meetings in a local grocery store parking lot and recruited two friends to join them. In one night they attacked four people in the same parking lot and stole hundreds of dollars from them.

Like most teenage criminals, the boys couldn't keep their mouths shut. Jaden thought his new stack of cash would impress girls at school, so he brought it with him the next day. School security had already suspected him of stealing phones at school, and they work closely with the city police. When a student shows up with a giant stack of money the day after four people are robbed by unidentified teenagers the case is pretty easy to solve. The police came to the school and questioned Jaden, who eventually admitted to being one of the Craiglist attackers. He then named all of his accomplices who were also arrested.

AFTERMATH

-Jermaine was arrested and sentenced as an adult. He is still in prison.

-Jaden served time in JDC but was eventually released and returned to Lincoln High.


Dice Games

The back alley dice games from movies and rap videos actually happen in Midwest City. Hundreds of dollars change hands in these bootleg craps games in the neighborhoods around LHS. Street gambling doesn't really attract the most upstanding citizens in Midwest City, and in many instances fights break out over misread dice or short changed pots.

Christian and Victor were fourth year students still sitting with sophomore level credits. Both had done time at alternative schools and in JDC, and both were known to associate with gang members in Midwest City. Early the school year the boys attended a craps game at an apartment complex in one of the most crime-ridden neighborhoods in town. The boys were with some older friends that were known gang members and some other older citizens with no known affiliation. After a few hours of drinking and smoking, everyone's judgement started to become hazy.

Xavier was a 22 year old upstart craps player who lived at the apartment complex hosting the game. That night he was on a hot streak and ended up winning more than $2000 from the other players. After the game everyone left peacefully, but some of the losers were a little angry. One of Christian and Victor's friends was especially upset and decided to head out to his car to get his gun. He returned to Xavier's apartment with Christian and Victor and banged on the door. When Xavier answered the three began arguing with him over the details of the game and demanded their money. Xavier refused, so the armed dice loser pulled his gun and shot Xavier, killing him on the spot. The three then fled the scene.

The next day Christian and Victor attended school as usual. Word had spread among the students that there was a murder the night before, but most LHS students didn't know Xavier. He had graduated from one of the other high schools in town and was in his 20s, so most students only knew that someone had been killed. The city police began rounding up the usual suspects. They learned what gang had been present at the dice game and started picking up members for questioning the next morning. Christian and Victor were both on the list to be picked up, so school security collected them from their classes. The police were quickly able to put together a picture of the murder. They knew who pulled the trigger and that Christian and Victor were both accomplices. They also were able to trace the shell casing and gun to a previous killing that had happened in Midwest City. The same gun was used to kill a 12 year old boy who was walking to a friend's house the year before. He was hit by a random bullet in a drive-by shooting. The murder of Xavier wouldn't have made real waves in the city. People killing each other over dice game arguments don't really make the news beyond the first week. That kind of crime is seen as business as usual in parts of

Midwest City. The killing of an innocent 12 year old in a drive-by however, was a big deal. The three involved were arrested and charged with murder.

AFTERMATH

> -Christian and Victor are in prison and will be for a long time. They will never return to Lincoln High.

"RIP Brandon"

Murder in Midwest City is sadly a common occurrence. Around 20 people are killed in violent crimes in the city each year. Some of the cases don't get much attention – like the shooting death of Xavier during a dice game argument. Most people don't seem to care if people with criminal backgrounds kill each other. There are a few cases each year that gain major attention. A husband killed his wife a few years ago and made national news because of the strange way he tried to cover it up. The killing of a young student will also always make the national news. Marvin was the 12 year old middle school student killed in a drive-by by the same people who killed Xavier, and his case made national news. The police stopped every car that came through the neighborhood where the shooting took place for weeks looking for leads. The case of Brandon was no exception to this rule.

Brandon was a freshman at LHS and a member of the freshmen football team. In October he was in his third month of high school. He hadn't gotten in trouble or been involved in anything besides football practice in his short high school career. On a Friday night in October he was hanging out with some friends. Two of them were sophomore members of the football team and like Brandon had a game Saturday morning at the school. Brandon and his friends Jamir, Ivan, and Coleton all decided to stay the night at a house near the school so they could walk over to their football game the next morning. The house was owned by Coleton's grandma, but it was also used by some of his cousins as their trap house. They sold drugs in the alley out back.

The four boys went to sleep Friday night but were woken up in the middle of the night by a pounding on the door. Coleton went to the door and answered. A couple of people he didn't recognize asked for his cousin, who wasn't there. Coleton told them this, closed the door, and went back to sleep. About an hour later the unknown people returned. This time they didn't knock, they just kicked in the door. Seven people rushed into the house and started shooting without warning. The four boys were startled awake and started scrambling for the back door. Brandon was hit and went down in the back yard. The other three were also hit but kept running. Ivan, Coleton, and Jamir all ran in different directions and were found passed out on different streets in the neighborhood. Brandon was still in the backyard and died before he was found. The seven shooters all escaped in different cars before police arrived.

Students at school the next week were in shock. The freshmen were all in mourning and no one really knew how to handle it. There were a lot of tears, but otherwise things were calm. The story made national news and the police worked the case around the clock until they found the people that broke in. All seven were arrested within a week. Five of them were former Lincoln High students who had dropped out and the other two were from out of town. All of them were known members of a gang and said they had been trying to rob the drug dealers that were usually at that house. All of them were charged with murder.

After Brandon's funeral there were peace marches and rallies around town to bring attention to the violence in the city. Older people from the community seemed outraged that something like this could happen, but in reality it happens all the time in Midwest City. A local rapper released a song called "RIP Brandon" as a tribute. In the music video students from the school and Brandon's family members appeared. The lyrics to the song expressed sadness over the death of Brandon, but they also glorified street violence and crime. The overall message of the song was that Brandon's world was a world of violence and death, and that we should for some reason celebrate this. The music video was a representation of the problems in Midwest City's community, and showed the challenge that Lincoln High School faces. Better schools could not have prevented Brandon from being murdered, but better schools could possibly reduce violence in the city if the efforts to change were strong enough.

## MIDWEST CITY SCHOOL SYSTEM

History

Midwest School District has served Midwest City for well over one hundred years, and the district has always reflected the city itself. If the city was prosperous, the district was producing graduates that went on to major universities and made national impacts. When the city became filled with crime and poverty, the district produced drop outs and graduates that attended no colleges afterwards.

The school district began with a few grade schools and added a high school, Lincoln High School, in the mid- to late-1800s. LHS served the entire city for about 50 years before a growing population of students necessitated the opening of two other high schools – Jefferson and Washington. These three high schools were all considered quality schools from the 1930s into the 1960s when changes in Midwest City started to hurt the school district. The population and demographic changes in Midwest City of the 1960s and 1970s stretched the city into surrounding unincorporated townships. One of these townships had its own high school, Roosevelt. Roosevelt was not large enough to sustain the huge influx of white flight residents into the township, so

Midwest City annexed the township, and the city school district annexed Roosevelt. Roosevelt became the premier high school in the district at this time. It also became the white high school in the district, while Jefferson and Lincoln High became all-black high schools. Washington was split evenly at about 50% of each race.

Throughout the 1980s and 1990s, the population of Midwest County continued to spread out from Midwest City's center. As the population continued to spread however, the district did not. New school districts appeared at the edges of town to cater to the richest and whitest people that could afford to move in to the newest neighborhoods in the area. These districts began draining Midwest City schools of students and of tax dollars.

By 2000, Midwest School District was operating with a budget deficit. The district had 40 schools to operate for thousands of students, but didn't have enough property tax income to fund everything. The state was also shorting the district money it was owed, making the problem even worse. The district had always operated under a neighborhood schools model. Students attended the grade school nearest to their house. Each major neighborhood had a grade school, so most students could stay local their entire school career.  There were 4 high schools, each in a different corner of the city.  This kept the city mostly divided into 4 regions without a lot of interaction.  A very small group of students were bussed from an all-black neighborhood near Jefferson to attend Roosevelt in order to provide a better balance of races, but otherwise most students attended the school nearest to them.  Budget problems made this system impossible to sustain.  Schools in the old neighborhoods of Midwest City were nowhere near capacity in the early 2000s.  Many of the buildings were over 100 years old and were falling apart, making them even more expensive to maintain.  The district created a plan to close 16 schools and consolidate student groups by busing students to other neighborhoods.

Mergers

The schools most affected by the mergers were the grade schools.  Thirteen grade school buildings around town were closed and merged with each other.  Three brand new buildings were built to replace three of the closed schools, but they were built double-size to accommodate students from other closed schools. The district had enough space for every student, so crowding wasn't an issue. Two middle schools were also closed and merged with nearby middle schools. These 15 grade and middle school closures definitely changed neighborhoods in Midwest City, but the closure of Washington High School had the greatest impact.

Washington was opened in the 1930s and served the eastern region of Midwest City. The neighborhoods near Washington were originally full of working class white families with factory jobs on the eastern side of town. The houses were small and not very expensive, but the streets were well kept. When the factories on the east side of town all shut down the neighborhood started to change. The working class families disappeared and were replaced by renters. Most people on the eastern side of town were renting their houses by the 1990s. The neighborhoods also began to decay. Buildings left vacant fell apart or burned down, and occupied houses even started to look terrible. Washington High School was originally built for 2500 students, but in 2000 it only had 1000. The district decided to close it and send most of the students to Lincoln High, which was also operating at about half capacity.

Lincoln High absorbed around 800 extra students in 2008. The school became very crowded and class sizes shot up to the mid-30s. The merger also brought together students from neighborhoods that were typically isolated from each other. Gangs from the central part of Midwest City around Lincoln High had existed for years and were rivals with gangs from the eastern part of town. Their high school aged members were now forced to attend the same school (when they showed up), and this created a tense situation. The police were called hundreds of times in the first year of the merger due to gang violence.

Present Day

Today, the district has 25 regular schools instead of 40. There are three high schools, eight middle schools, and fourteen grade schools. There are also a few alternative schools and special schools that only accept certain students. Students living in Midwest City can also attend two major religious school systems (Catholic and Lutheran) or a charter school in town. Their families can also move right outside of town and attend one of four school districts that share a border with Midwest City and are all very well-funded by property taxes. The Midwest School District budget looks better than it did in 2000, but they are still operating at a deficit.

Lincoln High has about 2000 high school aged students living within its boundaries. About 150 of those students chose to apply to a high level UP/WB program at Roosevelt and take a bus up to that school instead. About 200 other students go to the private high schools in town because they can afford the tuition. 50 students in the LHS area apply to the charter school in town and attend there. Finally, about 100 students are in alternative schools for behavior issues or in juvenile detention. This leaves Lincoln High with around 1500 kids each school year. The numbers constantly change, especially at the alternative schools and JDC, but they stick around 1500 at any given time.

Feeder Schools

Lincoln High students come from four feeder middle schools nearby – Grant, Jackson, Wilson, and Adams. All four of these middle schools are tough places for students and teachers. Students run wild through the halls and receive no discipline. Teachers kick students out constantly and nothing happens to them. The student scores are some of the lowest in the state. A "good day" at one of the LHS feeder schools is a day when bad kids don't show up and the rest of the kids sit quietly, probably not paying any attention to anything. These students show up as freshmen to LHS every year and have to be trained on how to act in a school as if they are kindergartners. They don't know how to sit in a desk, walk in a hallway, see a friend without slapping them, or talk to an adult. The biggest challenge at Lincoln High is taking a kid from one of our feeder middle schools and transforming them into an actual student before their behavior gets them suspended and expelled. The job seemed pretty much impossible, so Lincoln High got worse and worse until it finally reached "failed school" status in 2010.

## TEACHERS

It takes more than just bad students to make a school fail. As students got worse and worse the teachers at Lincoln High pushed them right along through. Total incompetence at every level of the staff at Lincoln High turned the building into a 7-hour-a-day holding cell instead of a school. The administrators stayed in their offices while the teachers did whatever they wanted. One teacher shared with me that he was never once observed by a principal during his first few years at Lincoln High, but each year he received an Outstanding evaluation with made up comments on the alleged rubric he was given. This kind of system turned good and decent teachers into slackers, and lazy slacker teachers into total jokes.

Mrs. Brown

Mrs. Brown was a long time Social Studies teacher at Lincoln High. Her schedule said she taught World History, but if you walked into her classroom at any given moment you would think she taught a Film Studies course. She showed at least 5 full length movies each quarter. Some of them were semi-related to history, but National Treasure starring Nic

Cage is not a documentary on the founding of the United States no matter how you present it to the class. Movies took up about 5 of the 9 weeks of each quarter, and during the other 4 weeks' worth of days Mrs. Brown sprinkled in notes and worksheets. Mrs. Brown had four kids at home and wasn't getting a lot of sleep, so when she gave notes she would put up a slide on the board and take a quick nap while her students wrote. She always told one of her good students to wake her up in 10 minutes when everyone was done copying. Using this system she was able to get her students to copy 5 slides while she took 5 quick power naps every class period. Mrs. Brown also loved to milk the school district for as much money as possible while doing as little work as she could.

Teacher attendance was very low at Lincoln High. At any given time there would be 2 or 3 teachers on "mental health" paid extended leave because they didn't want to deal with behaviors at LHS. On top of the long term absences, there would always be at least five other teachers out every single day. Some Fridays would have 10 to 15 teachers missing. Mrs. Brown didn't like to use her sick days though, so instead of calling off she developed a scheme with a few of her friends in the building. Teachers were paid to cover classes for absent teachers during their prep period. On a day she wanted to miss, Mrs. Brown would show up to work and teach her morning classes. She also had a morning meeting, but she would skip her meeting and sub a class instead. This earned her $25. She would then leave school early and have a friend cover her last class without telling anyone in payroll. This meant that she never lost a sick day, and she could pay her friend the $25 she had earned earlier in the day while skipping a meeting.

Mr. Black

Mr. Black was a Math teacher that was assigned to teach remedial math courses. His classes were full of students that couldn't pass Algebra or Geometry and could not continue through the math track. These students typically had low standardized test scores and had trouble paying attention in class. A lot of them also had behavior issues that went along with their inability to understand the material. When Mr. Black found out that he would be assigned to teach remedial math he didn't complain, he just decided to give up.  He came to work every day, but he never taught his class.

A new teaching philosophy called the "flipped classroom" was just becoming popular at that time, and Mr. Black decided that he would create his own version of the flipped classroom to avoid having to teach or even interact with his low level students.  He commandeered the math department laptop cart for his own daily use.  Every day he handed his students a worksheet with a website URL at the top.  The URL led to a video online that his students were supposed to watch.  The videos were just different math teachers giving example math lectures on different topics.  After watching the videos the students were supposed to answer questions on the worksheet.  Any time a student asked him a question he would say, "Go back and watch the video."  This was the only interaction he had with any of them.  At the end of a week he would give them a quiz or a test and if most of them failed he would just make them watch the same videos the next week.  This was his way of "re-teaching."  In a real flipped classroom the teacher is supposed to record themselves giving a lecture.  The students are supposed to watch the video on their own as homework and come to class to work on activities or projects. Mr. Black used the excuse that most of our students don't have the internet in order to do his modified flipped classroom where he did none of the work.

Mr. German

Mr. German was an assistant principal at another high school in the district. Roosevelt High had a reputation as an academically successful school where students took their classes seriously, and their staff was considered very competent. Mr. German was far from competent. He spent most of his day in his office. He never completed observations of any of his assigned teachers, and he let his referral stack fill to huge amounts before he did anything about them. While this might have been fine at Lincoln High, it was not acceptable at Roosevelt. The final straw came when the Roosevelt principal found Mr. German sleeping under his desk in his office during a school day like George Costanza.

Due to arcane hiring and firing rules governing the way districts remove staff, Mr. German could not be fired from his job. He had tenure from his time as a teacher, so he was at least partially safe. It's almost impossible to be fired if you have tenure in Midwest

School District. The best the district can do is demote and reassign incompetent teachers and administrators. An underperforming principal might be shifted over to an easy assignment like alternative school principal or demoted to assistant principal at a school with very few problems. Mr. German was already an assistant principal, so he was demoted back to teaching. He was given a choice of available openings in the areas he was certified in, one of which was Physical Education. Obviously seeking the easiest placement possible, Mr. German chose to be a PE teacher at Lincoln High. LHS had 5 PE teachers already, so Mr. German knew that there would be no pressure for him to manage a class. He could rely on the other PE teachers in the gym to do his job for him while he just hung out all day.

    Principals talk to each other, so when Mr. German showed up to Lincoln High everyone there already knew why he was let go from his assistant principal job at Roosevelt. The very first thing Mr. German said to his new boss was, "Where's my office?" From that moment on he did the bare minimum as a PE teacher. He let the other PE teachers discipline his students, and when he couldn't handle something he just called security. On the rare day when he had to cover the gym by himself, all hell would break loose. If Mr. German was the only PE teacher in the gym you could guarantee that at least two students would fight, two basketballs would be stolen, and one sex act would occur underneath the bleachers, though Mr. German swears that it couldn't have happened.

Mrs. Cross

Mrs. Cross was a member of the PE department alongside Mr. German. She was a veteran teacher in her last few years before retirement, so her main goal was coast to the end of her career while doing the least amount of work possible. She was always given a backup PE teacher to handle the girls in the gym, and her backup did everything for her, including taking attendance. She didn't even learn the students' names in her classes during her final years.

Teachers in this state can have a great retirement pension if they know what they are doing. When Mrs. Cross started teaching the retirement salary was calculated at 75% of the average salary made in the last three years teaching. Teachers could retire at age 55 or after 30 years teaching. The 75% was calculated based on the final total salary before taxes, including any extra pay received for things like coaching or extracurricular activities.  A teacher contemplating retirement always tried to add activities like these near the end of their career so they could make a better salary when retired.

At Lincoln High it was easy to become an activity sponsor or coach.  No one was interested in coaching small sports because the teams were always terrible and it was seen as too much work to turn the programs around.  The extracurricular activities were attended by very small groups of students, so it wasn't hard to manage groups like the 4 student chess team or the 8 student scholar bowl trivia team.  Mrs. Cross managed to become an assistant coach for girls' soccer and the head sponsor for the scholar bowl, despite knowing nothing about soccer and having no knowledge of academic trivia.  She collected large stipends simply because no one else wanted the jobs.

A new athletic director took over two years before Mrs. Cross's retirement.  She had already declared that she was retiring and the new AD decided to let her keep these coaching duties for two extra years just so he wouldn't mess up her retirement.  The girls' soccer team and scholar bowl teams won a grand total of zero games and matches with her in charge, but she still got her increased retirement check.

Ms. Baron

Ms. Baron was an Economics teacher in the Social Studies department. She came to Lincoln High in her 10$^{th}$ year as a teacher after being bumped around from school to school across the district. She had worked at all different levels teaching many different subjects, but was never kept around for more than a couple of years. No one wanted her, but no one could fire her. She was totally incompetent, but managed to gain tenure while teaching GED students at a night school run by the district, making her impossible to fire.

Ms. Baron was certified to teach several different subjects. She gained her multiple degrees through online courses from suspicious universities of questionable quality. She had a bachelor's degree in Social Studies teaching, a certification in Driver's Education, a certification in PE, a masters' in school administration with a principal's certification, and a masters' in English as a Second Language teaching. The district had a deal with teachers that would pay tuition for online courses, so Ms. Baron signed up for as many as possible.  She was then given raises upon completion, doubling the money she took from the district, despite no school actually wanting her as a teacher.

Lincoln High did not choose Ms. Baron. She was forced on them as the school she was at was closed. She was given an easy course to teach – senior Economics.  In senior Econ the students didn't learn actual economics; they learned how to balance a check book.  She also managed to get a job as the Behind the Wheel Driver's Ed teacher, earning her an extra $120 a day.

After a few months it was clear that Ms. Baron wasn't actually teaching anything in her economics classes. At department meetings each Social Studies teacher would share what they were currently teaching and she would always say "supply and demand."  In her 18 week course she claimed to have taught supply and demand every single week.  What she was really doing was bringing her students down to the computer lab to play a simulation game slightly related to economics.  She found the program browsing the internet and decided that it would be an easy way to blow a few weeks off of work.

The Lincoln High administration got wind of Ms. Baron's "teaching" and attempted to remove her, but her tenure prevented it. The best they could do was reassign her to a position where she couldn't do as much damage. They assigned her to be an ESL co-teacher since she had the degree. Even though she only spoke English, she was given a schedule in classrooms with Spanish speaking students who needed translations. To make sure that the Spanish kids didn't fail every class, the school also hired a Spanish speaking aide to act as Ms. Baron's assistant. Ms. Baron is now free to arrive 10 to 15 minutes late to every class because she can't speak Spanish anyway; her aid just covers for her. When she gets to class she just sits in the back on her cell phone playing games or checking Facebook, all while collecting a paycheck.

The Interventionists

Bad teachers are a major problem at Lincoln High, and their removal is difficult. Instead of removing them the school found ways to get them away from students by giving them easy jobs for the same salary. One of those jobs created for incompetent teachers was called "Instructional Interventionist." This title was given to three failed teachers at Lincoln High in the same year.  They were given an office and a vague assignment that allowed them to do whatever personal projects they wanted.  None of the projects they worked on had much of an impact, but at least they weren't running a classroom.

   Mrs. Trotts was an old English teacher who really needed to retire, but didn't have the years of service yet.  She used old school methods and her main strategy for getting students to pay attention was by yelling "This is important!" over and over again.  When an interventionist position became available she was shifted over to it.  She had two jobs for the entire school year.  Her main assignment was to help teachers create rubrics for grading writing assignments.  This could have been valuable, but instead of working with teachers she just printed off a rubric used by the state to grade the writing portion of the 8th grade state-wide standardized test.  If a teacher disagreed with the rubric, she would shout at them until they agreed to use it.  Her other assignment was standardized test coordinator.  These tests happened three times a year and lasted two weeks each, so for six weeks each school year she had to sit in a computer lab with students and administer a test.  This was all she did for years at Lincoln High until she retired.

Mrs. James was a former math teacher who couldn't handle disruptive students.  If too many students were disruptive she would appear on the verge of breakdown and call off work the next day.  It just wasn't working for her, so she was assigned to be an interventionist.  Her assignment was the exact same as Mrs. Trotts's except she worked with math teachers on word problem rubrics.  That was all she had to do to earn a year's salary.

Mrs. Jacobs was a former science and special ed teacher who everyone called "The Tornado."  She had an in-your-face approach to student discipline and was constantly in arguments with them, so she was assigned a job as an interventionist.  Her self-selected roles were school paperwork manager and ACT prep tutor for student athletes.  All she did in a given day was call down one or two students an hour out of their PE class and go over ACT test material with them.  She only worked with football or basketball players because her sons played football. No other students ever saw Mrs. Jacobs.

Mrs. Gerald

Mrs. Gerald was a Chemistry teacher with a flair for the dramatic. She didn't really know how to talk to teenagers and treated every minor situation like it was life-or-death. If a student lied to her about why they were late to class she would try to start a full-fledged investigation into their whereabouts by asking for cameras to be checked and passes to be time stamped. Relaxing was not possible for Mrs. Gerald.

A family of four students from India moved to Midwest City and spoke very little English. Rakesh and Sanjay both had Mrs. Gerald for Chemistry, but they couldn't really communicate with her at all. There was a co-teacher in all of their classes, but she only spoke Spanish and English, so she couldn't really talk to them either. She was able to communicate with them through Google translate apps on their phones, but otherwise conversations were very limited. Mrs. Gerald didn't really seem to notice or care about this, so she continued teaching them as if they were any other English speaking students.

One day Mrs. Gerald walked into her class and saw Rakesh and Sanjay standing in the doorway of the chemical closet in the back of her classroom. She asked them what they were doing back there, but they didn't respond. All they heard was a white lady yelling nonsense at them, so they didn't say anything. Mrs. Gerald then went back into her chemical closet and somehow noticed that a few chemicals were missing. Despite a lack of an inventory to prove they were missing or a lock on the door, Mrs. Gerald immediately blamed Rakesh and Sanjay for the supposed theft.

There is a procedure teachers follow when they learn of a theft in their classroom. If something minor like school supplies are stolen, they just tell the kids to grow up and give back whatever was taken. If a phone or something valuable is taken the teacher can talk to the kids to try to see who has it. A lot of times this works, and the stolen items will be returned. If not, the next step would be to place a call to school security. They would come down and search involved students or search every student if needed. Nine out of ten times this solves a theft in the classroom. Mrs. Gerald was not one for procedure or for calm solutions to issues. When Mrs. Gerald didn't get an answer from the boys she could have asked her co-teacher for help, but she didn't.

She could have picked up the phone and called for school security, but she didn't do that either. Instead, she picked up her cell phone and dialed 911. She reported Rakesh and Sanjay for stealing chemicals and accused them of plotting to construct a bomb with them. The police didn't know Mrs. Gerald, so they had to take the call seriously. About 10 city officers and detectives arrived at school with bomb kits. They cordoned off the science hallway and conducted a search of every student in that area. After the show was over they ended up finding nothing. The boys hadn't taken anything at all; Mrs. Gerald just didn't have an inventory and didn't know what was in her chemical closet to begin with. To this day no one knows why Mrs. Gerald leapt from missing chemicals to bomb threat, but she probably mistook the Indian boys for Middle Easterners and assumed they were terrorists.

Whether induced by her shame or just another random incident, Mrs. Gerald worked for a few more weeks before slipping on a piece of paper in class. Her resulting "injuries" forced her to take a long medical leave from work, though she did eventually return with stories of her horrible fall.

Mr. Graves

Mr. Graves was a Lincoln High graduate from the 1990s who returned to teach Algebra at his alma mater.  He believed that the glory days of Lincoln High were still a reality, and that students needed to act like they did when he was in school or get out.  In some ways his ideas weren't wrong, but his presentation of his ideas left people wondering why he was even a teacher.  At any chance he got he would complain about how he hated his students and how they always bothered him with questions.  Many teachers would see answering questions about content as part of their job, but it only made Mr. Graves angry.  Every question he got he assumed they should already know the answer to, so he just yelled that back at his students every time.  His style was confrontational to the extreme.  Making fun of kids, belittling them, one-upping them, and using complete sarcasm were the only ways he talked to them.  In addition to his terrible attitude towards students, he had anger issues and could easily be set off at school.  He would frequently go into shouting rants at his classes as if that would help them learn math better.

One day Mr. Graves had reached his limit. He had graded quizzes the night before and his students had performed poorly. Every single student received a 'D' or an 'F' on his quiz, so of course he blamed them for not living up to his 1993 standards. "Back in my day, you did the homework, you came to class, you sat down, you shut up, and you learned math!" he told his class. Some students got aggressively defiant when Mr. Graves talked like that to them. They would immediately start cussing him out, but he didn't have a problem with those students. He just threw them out and failed them. Mr. Graves's real problem was students who wanted to learn but just didn't get it. The day after everyone failed his quiz a girl asked him to explain what she had done wrong. He started up his rant about the good old days, and when she saw her question wasn't going to be answered, she asked if she could retake the quiz. The word "retake" triggered Mr. Graves. His eyes grew wide and his brain started flying as he tried to come up with something to shout about the problem with retakes. The steam built too quickly, and Mr. Graves couldn't contain himself. He let out a primal scream as he punched the whiteboard in front of his class. The white board, being mounted to a wall, didn't give, but Mr. Graves's hand did. He left a blood streak on his board, but he was gone in an instant.

Mr. Graves went to the school nurse but was noticed as he passed through the office. He was forced to go to the hospital for stitches on his hand and to take a drug test. He passed the test, though he probably needed a Xanax. When he returned to school he faced no disciplinary action and was allowed to continue teaching the next day. That quarter he failed 95 of his 140 students, a school wide record for 'F's.

Mr. Danes

Mr. Danes was a Chemistry teacher alongside Mrs. Gerald. Mr. Danes took an approach to teaching like a drill instructor takes an approach to boot camp. He didn't want students to cause disruptions in his class, and he didn't believe that disruptive students should be allowed to stay in his room. The problem was that his definition of a disruption was much smaller than what the administration considered a discipline worthy disruption. If a student talked once while he was talking he would eject them. If a student looked at their cell phone once he would eject them. Neither of these offenses warranted further discipline from the assistant principals, so students he kicked out would be back in class within five minutes.

Mr. Danes loved undermining the administration, so he came up with a plot to make students he considered problems get stronger consequences. Instead of kicking out a student right away for disruption, he would approach them and try to embarrass them. He would call them names in front of his classes. His goal was to anger the disruptive student to push them to do something more serious. Some students would leave it there, but others would take public ridicule as a challenge. Many would cuss him out instantly. This was something the administration could suspend a student for, so Mr. Danes loved getting cussed out. If he got a kid to cuss him out he could guarantee they would miss the next day of his class at least.

Escalating a situation at Lincoln High is easy. Some students are capable of violence and many have no problem cussing out their teachers. Mr. Danes used this approach daily in his class, but for one student in particular he thought it wasn't enough. Jason was a pest who loved to chat through class and draw attention to himself. He would sometimes fall for Mr. Danes' bait and cuss him out, but most of the time he would just keep clowning. One day Mr. Danes got frustrated that Jason wouldn't cuss him out, so he decided to cuss first. Mr. Danes told Jason that his behavior was "bullshit" and that he needed to start "acting like a human being if he wanted to get anywhere in life." Jason could handle being singled out in front of the class because he enjoyed attention, but he couldn't handle being called a failure in front of everyone. He stood up and Mr. Danes got directly in his face. The two started screaming at each other until Mr. Danes challenged Jason to hit him. Mr. Danes shouted "are you going to hit me?" over and over again at Jason until a teacher from the next classroom came in with security and separated them. Neither of them faced any disciplinary action.

Ms. Gilmore

Ms. Gilmore was an English teacher who tried to create an image that she was the "most caring teacher in the school." She was always going the extra mile to help out students with their school work and personal life problems. Sometimes she was a little over the top with her "helpfulness." She would buy food for her classes weekly, she would drive students home from school, and she would buy them expensive electronics like Beats headphones for winning contests in class.  She wanted to be her students' best friend, and she also wanted to be the next Freedom Writers teacher, but what she ended up being was a child predator and accused criminal.

    Ms. Gilmore wanted personal relationships with all of her students.  She would talk to them about their dating lives and get their phone numbers to text them after hours.  Obviously, not all students can maintain a professional relationship with an adult, so some of them took her interest in them to mean she wanted to date them.  The problem was that she actually did want to date them.  Somehow she became mentally warped and believed that in order to help kids she could have intimate relationships with them.  She was reported to the administration by several teachers for inappropriate relationships with students, but nothing could ever be proven.  She was informally investigated several times and no evidence could ever be found.  Everyone in the building suspected her of something, but no one knew what.  Eventually word leaked that she was having sex with a student and she was called in for questioning by the police.  They arrested her and charged her, but all five students she allegedly had relationships refused to speak. One boy would openly brag at school about having sex with her, but refused to talk to the police, so she was released. The district forced her to resign because she didn't have tenure, but all of her charges were dropped. She is currently dating a Lincoln High graduate who was one of her students in her first year teaching.

Other Teachers

While the previously discussed teachers are the worst Lincoln High had to offer, the rest of the staff was far from stellar. Most teachers at Lincoln High would not have made it in a different school. All of them somehow found their way to one of the worst schools in the state and did their best to make it even worse.

Mr. Simmons was an English teacher who would get mad at his students for minor disruptions and stop teaching in the middle of class. He would tell them to figure everything out on their own. Eventually his classes drove him to quit in the middle of the year.

Mrs. Burgess was a freshman English teacher who only pretended to teach. She let her special education co-teacher run every class every day.

Mr. Franklin was a Remedial Reading teacher who specialized in writing detailed referrals. He considered any minor infraction to warrant a dissertation length essay to be written up as a referral.

Mrs. Sears was an Art teacher who took frequent mental health vacations. One week she spent her sick leave skiing in Colorado where she faked a knee injury and called off the rest of the year.

Mr. Beltran was a Spanish teacher who believed that even his freshmen should be fluent. When they weren't he cussed at them in Spanish and threw them out of class.

Mr. King was another Spanish teacher who believed that showing the Spanish versions of Disney movies with English subtitles was a valid teaching method.

Ms. Grable was a special education teacher who protested her assignment to teach remedial English because she couldn't read and understand the stories.

Mrs. Edgars was a French teacher who used up every sick day she had. She called in sick one day because she had woken up late and wanted to "reset her sleep schedule" and "try again tomorrow."

Mr. Simms was a Chorus teacher who wore sweatpants to work every day because "technically there is no teacher dress code."

Ms. Scott was an English teacher who threw a fit when she saw she was assigned a co-teacher that she wasn't friends with. She whined daily until the principal made a change.

Mr. Ritenour was a History teacher who set the record for most referrals written in one year. Forgetting a pencil in his class was grounds for an ejection and referral.

Mr. Petrich was a History teacher who quit the day before school started because of the "working conditions" at the school. I was hired to replace him.

Mrs. Theodore was a History teacher who sold homemade baked goods out of the closet in her room to supplement her own personal income.

Mrs. Jenkins was a math teacher who hated the Lincoln High students so much that she just didn't show up for work after Winter Break. She never returned.

Mrs. Summers was a special education co-teacher who brought her iPad to school every day and watched her favorite TV shows instead of teaching.

Mr. Johnson was a math teacher who sent suggestive texts to a female student, but said "it was okay because I'm a good Christian and would never act on it."

Mr. Tardis was a Science teacher who arrived every day at 8:00 and headed straight for the copy room. His first class also started at 8:00. He spent the first 20 minutes of every day making giant packets of worksheets on the copiers for his other classes while occasionally popping in on his 1st hour.

Teacher Evaluations

When Lincoln High reached failed school status, almost every teacher in the building was rated as an Outstanding or Capable teacher according to their evaluations. If you asked any of them what was wrong at Lincoln High they would say that it was the students. The students were 100% terrible and the teachers had nothing to do with it.

In reality the evaluation system was a total joke that didn't require teachers to do anything to be rated at a good level. A teacher who could keep their students under control and never caused problems with administrators was rated Outstanding, and a teacher with a pulse was rated Capable. The only teachers that were fired were those that actually committed crimes at work. Principals weren't really required to document their observations, so they just made them up. They knew they would have a hard time hiring people at a failed school, so they kept their teacher ratings high so no one would get fired. All this did was guarantee that bad teachers would get tenure and be impossible to remove if someone ever came along and tried to fix things.

## PART 2 – TURNAROUND

In the 2010-2011 school year Lincoln High School bottomed out. The school reached the bottom of every statistical category that schools can be ranked in. At the end of that school year a math teacher compiled a report showing all of these statistics. His report became known as the McGee Report and spread around the district. When district administration saw the report they finally acknowledged that something was wrong and needed to be done. The problems seemed insurmountable, but the district had to find someone to do something about it besides taking a nap in their office and ignoring it. The district found an energetic young assistant principal in one of the middle schools in town and chose him for promotion to Lincoln High principal. Mr. Everett began working early that summer with a few teachers from the building on his plan to turn around the school.

## YEAR 1

The first step in their plan was to acknowledge the huge list of problems at the school. In short, the school had problems with administration, teachers, teacher evaluations, students, parents, the community, crime, and even the building. A plan had to be put in place over the summer to fix all of them. A small group of teachers met daily with Mr. Everett and started the huge process. They realized that it was impossible to fix any of them without a few concessions from the district and the union. They also needed a bunch of money to make any of their ideas work. Mr. Everett met with the union president and the superintendent and asked them for a Multilateral Agreement, a special side contract that basically let him do whatever he wanted at Lincoln High without interference from district level administrators or union officials. They district only agreed to the MA on the condition that they could veto it later if anything horrible happened. The union only agreed with the MA on the condition that any teacher Mr. Everett wanted to replace could have a job secured somewhere else in the district.

Mr. Everett was able to secure power over the turnaround process with the MA, but the district still had no money to give him to make his plan work. He got together with his small teacher leader group again and wrote a grant with them. The school was approved for a three year eight million dollar grant from the federal government. The money could be used for anything related to school improvement, but in exchange Mr. Everett and the teachers had to give some authority to a consulting group that would oversee the money and guide the turnaround process. The Center for Educational Progress sent a consultant to work full time at Lincoln High and had two other consultants make regular appearances to check on things. The CEP had good connections to necessary Professional Development to help the school, but they were also just working to build their own firm's name as an ed consulting powerhouse.

HIRING

    Lincoln High had a reputation around town, so Mr. Everett knew what he was walking into. He knew the stories of the students and more importantly the staff. The MA he had secured gave him some freedom in hiring that most new principals don't get. An all new group of assistant principals was brought in, giving the school a new administration. Mr. Everett was also allowed to remove 50% of the teachers in the building, but the rest he had to keep. Every teacher previously mentioned in the TEACHERS section still worked at Lincoln High after Mr. Everett removed half of the staff. That means that whoever he cut was even worse than a guy who punched his white board in rage or a woman who slept at her desk while her kids took notes.

To replace the missing teachers Mr. Everett began recruiting teachers from around the district and recent college graduates. He was able to convince successful teachers from other schools to join him at LHS and he managed to hire a large group of new young teachers. He had to do this to gain staff support. The people he brought in had to be willing to try new things, so he handpicked teachers that he thought could change the school.

## ADMIN CHANGES

The new team of administrators at LHS had to change the way they evaluated teachers and the way they handled discipline. The old school assistant principal was more like a dean. They just added up points as each student got a referral. If a student got too many points they could be asked to serve a detention after school. The new system at LHS required assistant principals to actually talk to the students who got in trouble. It also required them to leave their office sometimes to observe teachers.

## TEACHER CHANGES

Teachers had to totally change their mindset when it came to teaching at Lincoln High. What they had been doing before couldn't even really be defined as teaching. Some teachers would show up and try to lecture about content to their students, but this only worked for a few teachers who were entertaining enough to hold the students' attention. Most teachers just showed up and passed out worksheets or assigned sections from the textbook. There was no real interaction, and students' grades were just a point bank where they made deposits by submitting worksheets.

### The New Teaching Model

The new Lincoln High teaching model was a total reworking of what had been considered teaching before. It started with planning. Every academic subject teacher was given one less class to teach each day. During that period they were assigned to department meetings called PLCs where they had to work with their department teammates in creating curriculum. The curriculums had to be designed using Universal Core standards and planned in reverse. Teachers had to spend weeks writing tests before they could plan any lessons. The CEP consultant group provided guidance in how to actually use standards and write tests, because most teachers at Lincoln High had never done either. A standard was an unknown concept at the old Lincoln High, and tests were printed from test banks provided with the teacher's edition of each textbook.

Once standards were chosen and tests were written, teachers had to plan long term units and daily lessons with each other. No one could go off and teach whatever they wanted any more, all courses had to align with each other. One US History teacher couldn't spend an extra month on the Revolutionary War just so he could show The Patriot while another US History teacher spent an extra week on the Cold War just so he could show Red Dawn. Everyone had to be on the same topic at all times, and no one was supposed to show full length movies.

The new lesson plans being made were very complex at first, especially for teachers who weren't used to planning anything at all. Teachers had to make sure that everything they did aligned to the standards they had chosen and the tests they had written. They also had to use new strategies that they were trained on over the summer. Part of the eight million dollar grant went to providing every teacher with training in a huge amount of strategies that they could use to engage students who didn't care about school.

Every teacher was first trained on how to teach students to improve their reading and writing. Most incoming students at Lincoln High were way behind in all academic areas. The average reading level of an incoming freshman in 2011 was below 6th grade. Most teachers didn't know what to do about it, so they just taught high school like they were teaching middle school. The school hired a reading and writing specialist to show LHS teachers how to take high school level texts and writing prompts and make it so students at any reading level could handle them.

Reading and writing are boring. Most students in Midwest City don't want to read Shakespeare or Thomas Jefferson. 140 characters is the maximum length allowed on Twitter, and that's the limit of most of their reading interest. In the first year under the new system there wasn't much success. Teachers planned better, but students were the same. A kid who disrupts, disrespects, fights, or sleeps through class won't notice if their teacher has better lesson plans. The first year changes were behind the scenes, unnoticed by students, but they laid the groundwork for the transformation. In addition to removing bad teachers and training the rest how to plan and teach reading and writing, there were many other changes in the first year:

-No more assignments that involved just reading a section of a textbook and answering the questions in the back.

-No more memorization only tests.

-No more weekly worksheet packets.

-No more time wasters like crossword puzzles or word finds.

-No more "free days".

-No more movies.

-No more winging it.

-No more arriving to work right as school was starting.

Grading Policy

One of the more controversial changes implemented by Mr. Everett was a new grading policy. The old policy was the system used in most schools. Missing assignments were scored as a 0% and anything from 0% to 59% was an 'F'. At Lincoln High, missing work is a huge problem. Even the best students didn't do homework, and half of the students wouldn't even do classwork.  The grading system guaranteed that students who didn't do homework were going to fail, even if they could pass tests and quizzes.

The new system removed all grades below 40%.  If a student didn't do an assignment, their teacher had to give them a 40 instead of a 0.  If a student failed an assignment at a grade lower than 50%, they were automatically given a 50.  The only true 'F's were between 50 and 59.  In effect it gave 40 free points to students who did nothing, but they still failed.  The true purpose was to make the range of 'F' grades the same as the range for every other letter grade.  It made it possible for students who were failing to more easily recover their grades and reach a passing level.  They would still have to do the work, but they would actually have a chance to reach success instead of just giving up.

The other major grading policy change was retakes.  If students got a 'D' or an 'F' on a quiz or a test they had to be given the option to retake it and recover some of their points.  It was up to the teacher to create alternative forms if they wanted to, but they had to give second chances.

The second chance and 40/50 'F' rule philosophies were hard to accept for a lot of teachers. Some teachers had public fits in meetings about them; others refused to follow them, and most hated them privately. When being presented these two changes most teachers in most school would probably disagree with them initially. But once teachers embraced the idea that people deserve second chances, it became a lot easier to handle.

Relationships

It's sometimes tough for teachers to relate to students like the ones at Lincoln High. Most teachers have a very different background from the students at LHS. Even the LHS teachers who were LHS alumni grew up in a different era. Mr. Everett saw this problem and thought that it would have to be fixed if LHS was to become a successful school. A short class was built in to every student's schedule called Advisory. Every teacher was assigned an Advisory of about 20 students. There was no curriculum they had to follow, they just had to get to know the 20 students and mentor them through their academic classes. The idea was that every student should have an adult in the building they knew and could talk to, so that problems like massive brawls created by drama could be prevented. LHS still has massive brawls brought on by drama, but there is a lot less of it than there was before Advisory.

RESULTS

After the first year the results weren't great. Teachers improved their planning and interactions with students, but the actual numbers that mattered didn't change. Student attendance, scores, and behaviors were still horrible. Referrals went down significantly, but that was mostly a result of better teachers who knew how to handle disruptive students before a referral needed to be written. There were still major fights, and even a 50% reduction in referrals still meant over 10,000 were written. Almost all of the stories from this book took place in years one and two. The greatest impact year one had was that the staff started to notice that the old style of teaching wasn't going to be possible at LHS anymore. A lot of older teachers transferred, retired, or straight up quit because they decided that year one wasn't worth the effort.

## YEARS 2 and 3
### TEACHER CHANGES

The first year was practice. Mr. Everett and his new staff needed to see if it was even possible to change teaching methods of old school teachers and change students who hated school. The very small successes showed them that it was possible, so in the second year more changes were added on to try to reach actual success.

Over the summer even more young teachers were recruited and hired as older staff members decided to leave the school. The new teachers looked at the work done in year one and worked to add and improve for the next year. A new evaluation system was also piloted to improve teacher ability instead of just assigning them made up ratings.

### PLC

Every core academic teacher had a PLC meeting in their daily schedule. In year one they were almost all used for the creation of common tests and unit plans. In year two, the purpose of the teacher PLCs began to change. The meetings became reflection and critique sessions in which teachers helped each other improve. Teachers were required to bring in their lesson plans and their student work to show the rest of their department.  They also took turns filming their lessons and brought video to PLC.  Once a week a different teacher brought their plans, work, and a video.  They were then critiqued by the rest of their department.

The video aspect of PLC caused an uproar just as the grading policy change had, but teachers eventually got over it.  There was no secret camera installed in every classroom, so teachers had the freedom to bring whatever video they wanted.  All they had to worry about was having at least one good thing happen in the course of week.  If they couldn't manage that then their video would be bad, but they probably shouldn't have been teaching anyway.

Freshmen House

Another major change in year two was the creation of a freshmen house.  The "house" concept isolated the freshmen to one hallway of the school where they had all of their major classes.  The teachers in the freshmen house would teach freshmen classes all day and work closely with each other on improving their students' behavior and academics.  Young energetic teachers who were willing to do the hardest job in the school were selected for the freshmen house. Most incoming freshmen at LHS were way behind on academics and had no idea how to behave in school, so the job wasn't for the older teachers who weren't willing to try new strategies. No matter how much progress the school made the freshmen teachers always had to start their year with unprepared students.

The freshmen class at Lincoln High always had the majority of the behavior problems. Over 50% of the referrals written at the school were written for freshmen. There was also a large amount of repeat freshmen in the building. Repeat freshmen passed none of their classes the first time around and were retaking them all. The repeating freshmen made the job of freshmen house teachers almost impossible. They would behave even worse than they had the first time around because they were in all of the same classes they took the year before, but with younger students they could try to impress with their clown-like behavior. The students couldn't be expelled from LHS because they didn't do enough to warrant it, but they still caused major disruptions in all of their classes. The school spent a lot of grant money trying to find ways to solve this problem, and finally they found a solution.

Alternative School within a School

LHS needed somewhere to place the most unprepared freshmen who did absolutely nothing in class besides cause disruptions. Some of them fought and could be expelled for it, but most of them just cussed out their teachers, screamed at no one, listened to music seven hours a day, and did no school work. They would fail every class in their freshmen year and come right back the next year and do the same. Mr. Everett's team decided that these students needed to be separated out and placed in very small classes on their own where they couldn't disrupt students who might actually be trying to learn.

The district owned a small building across the street from the main Lincoln High building, so the building was repurposed as "Lincoln East," an alternative school within Lincoln High. Lincoln East was created for any freshman who had more referrals than credits by the end of their first year in high school. The 50 worst freshmen were selected to be moved across the street where they had classes only with each other and never got to see the main campus.  Students on the main campus could be sent over to Lincoln East at either the end of a semester or school year if they failed to earn any credits.

Lincoln East was one of the greatest successes of the turnaround process.  Freshmen classes are still tough in the first semester of school, but they could be much worse with repeaters.  After the first semester freshmen can either gain maturity or be sent to Lincoln East.  The removal of these students makes the class environment on the main campus much calmer and allows teachers to teach instead of discipline.

Over at East, four teachers have one of the toughest jobs in the school.  They have all of the worst students, but they have very small class sizes and a lot of freedom on how they can maintain discipline.  Students can be sent back and forth at any time between teachers if they are having a problem in one class.  They can work on the computer to recover missing credits.  The entire system is set up to allow them to earn their way back to the main campus.  Those that actually care will try harder than they ever have to earn that privilege.  Those that don't care still act the way they always did, but they don't destroy the learning environment in the same way they used to be able to.

Teacher Evaluations

The old teacher evaluation system had some major problems. It was totally subjective and didn't require anything more than general evidence to justify the rating of teachers. Most teachers were rated "Outstanding" even in a school that had failed. The eight million dollar grant that Mr. Everett applied for required that he use a new evaluation method on his teachers. The new method, called the Albertson Model, required that teachers be rated in 5 categories using detailed rubrics. Administrators would be required to visit each teacher's classroom six times in a school year to gather evidence in each of the categories. Within each category a teacher could receive ratings of "Inadequate," "Needs Development," "Capable," or "Outstanding." All five category ratings were then averaged together to create an overall rating. Teachers with an Outstanding or Capable were safe, but teachers with Needs Development or Inadequate ratings could be let go at any time by the school.

The new five categories teachers were rated in were Planning, Environment, Instruction, Professionalism, and Student Growth. It took hours to learn the rubric, so teachers were given PLC time to learn how to master it. What had to be done to reach Outstanding was pretty straightforward, but probably impossible at Lincoln High. To reach Outstanding levels in Environment and Instruction teachers had to have their students running their classes. They had to create lessons that let the students take the lead while the teachers sat back and moderated. This is possible in a great school, but it seemed pretty tough at Lincoln High. No teacher would want to let the wild students in their classes have total control, so in the beginning most teachers shot for being Capable instead.

The Student Growth category of the evaluation caused the most problems. Teachers were rated based on how many points their students improved on tests. English and Math teachers were required to give a standardized test to their students in September and January. If enough of their students improved their scores they would be rated as Outstanding teachers in that category. The standardized test was graded in a way that made it very difficult for a student to improve their score by more than a few points.  Every other teacher was allowed to write their own test to measure their students' growth.  History and Science teachers just used tests they had written with their departments.  Their students were also only required to improve their scores for their teachers to be rated Outstanding.  This means that a student could get a 51% (F) on their test in September and score a 52% (F) on the same test in January and still be counted as having improved.  History and Science teachers had a much easier time improving their students' scores than English and Math teachers.  Most teachers in History and Science had 100% of their students grow, so they were always given an Outstanding in that category.  Other teachers could pretty much do anything to measure their students' growth.  PE teachers could have their students run a mile in September and then run a faster one in January.  Art teachers could have their students draw a picture in September and then draw a better one in January.

    The new evaluation system took a lot of work to implement, and required teachers to do a lot more than they ever had.  It made most teachers improve just by forcing them to think about everything on the rubrics. The data though, showed that the new evaluation system was basically the same as the old one. Administrators tried to use the new rubrics faithfully, but student growth ratings gave almost every teacher a boost. In the end, teachers who probably should have been rated as Needs Development were given Capable ratings because they received a boost from their students' inflated growth scores.

## RESULTS

After two more years in the new system, things did actually start to improve. Most teachers tried to improve their teaching by reflecting and sharing in PLC. Student scores on standardized tests actually went up, attendance improved, and referrals went down by another 50%. There were actually less fights and major disruptions in year three once the worst students were relocated across the street to Lincoln East. A majority of the students seemed to be buying into the new program and were starting to care more about their grades than causing drama.

## YEARS 4 and 5

The eight million dollar grant lasted three years. Lincoln High was supposed to fix all of its problems in three years, or at least set up a system that would last beyond the money. Year four was a test to see if the system could survive. Mr. Everett saved some of the money by paying in advance for one additional training session that would improve teaching.

The last piece of the puzzle was engagement. Teachers knew how to improve the reading and writing level of students, improve their math scores, and build relationships, but most classrooms at Lincoln High were operating in a teacher-led environment. Before year four every teacher was trained in how to create student-led activities so that engagement in learning could be increased.

Lincoln High continued to grow through years four and five and is still slowly improving. Every year teachers get better at the system that was created. Students still come to LHS as unprepared freshmen, but the teachers at the freshmen level have been able to quickly train most of them to be more mature. Today almost every teacher in the building has a handle on in-class behavior. Students still try to disrupt classes, but teachers know how to handle it without kicking them out. Fights still happen in the hallways, but some of them are totally unavoidable. Security and administrators work to monitor drama and try to make interventions. Sometimes interventions work, but other times students say they are over it and fight the next day anyway.

## PART 3 - RESULTS

FAILURE

The data at Lincoln High looks great, but only if you look at the growth that has occurred. LHS students still score well below the state average on standardized tests. The average ACT score for juniors at LHS went from around a 14 to around a 19. That's a great improvement, but a 19 won't get students into many colleges. The school also has more referrals and suspensions than similar high schools. Discipline data has been reduced by more than 75%, but a reduction from 20,000 referrals to 5,000 referrals in a year still leaves LHS with more than most schools. The school still has lazy teachers who have actually become even better at being lazy by finding ways to avoid doing all of the new things they are being asked to do.

There are too many outside factors that good reform at Lincoln High cannot control. When students arrive as 9th graders at LHS they are always totally unprepared. The feeder schools that send students to Lincoln High have no discipline and no academics. They all look like Lincoln High did 5 years ago. They don't have good enough leadership or enough teachers willing to make the necessary changes in their buildings, so the students they send to LHS are behind.

The Midwest City community itself is still full of poverty and crime. Five years of reform at a single high school in town can't fix this no matter how big the government grant is. Our students live in violent neighborhoods where they see things that students in other schools don't grow up seeing. Many of Lincoln High's students have had their houses broken into and they have all seen street fights. Their parents are from this community, and many of them attended Lincoln High at a time when the school was terrible. LHS students are raised in a broken community, and Lincoln High teachers have four years to bring them up to the standards of the rest of the country.

The state government has also made it difficult to fix Lincoln High. There are three laws that were passed under the guise of "progressive education reform," but that actually make it impossible to make progress. It is a state law that teachers be measured based on the growth of their students on tests, but the tests are incredibly easy for students to show growth on, so teachers are given inflated ratings. There is another state law that prevents special education students from being suspended for more than ten days in a school year and makes it almost impossible for them to be expelled.  Even special ed students with criminal records can commit violent acts at school without the threat of expulsion.  The third state law that was passed will go into effect next school year. The latest law makes it more difficult to suspend all students for their behavior.  Students will only be able to be suspended for extreme actions like fighting, but not for more "minor" actions like cussing out a teacher.  Without the threat of suspension this could lead to an increase in these behaviors.

Lincoln High's Turnaround Failures:

- Students are still performing below average compared to the rest of the country.
- Teachers are still finding ways to be lazy and avoid doing their jobs.
- The teachers' union still protects bad teachers from removal.
- LHS feeder schools are still failures.
- Parents are still hard to find at Lincoln High events.
- The Midwest City community is still full of crime and violence.
- The state government has several laws that make it difficult to improve schools.

SUCCESS

If you walked into a Lincoln High classroom before the grant, you would've seen a class of thirty students and one teacher. Ten of the students would have been on their phones texting while listening to music on their headphones. Ten of them would have been carrying on a loud conversation about yesterday's fight. Five of them would have been sleeping, and the other five would have been working silently on a worksheet that the teacher had passed out at the start of class.

If you walked into a Lincoln High classroom today, you would still see a class of thirty students and one teacher. Twenty-four of them would have been working together in small groups trying to solve a hands-on problem. Two of them would have been on their phones, two of them would have been having an irrelevant conversation, and two of them would have been sleeping.

The school has improved in the five years since its failure. Most of the students in the building come to school ready to work. Almost all of the teachers try to plan lessons that engage their students and force them to work together to solve problems. Most students solve their personal problems at home, or talk to their teachers about them. Almost all students check their grades religiously and want to know what it will take to get to the next level. The school has shown more statistical growth in every important category than every other school in the district.

Lincoln High's Turnaround Successes:
　-The school environment has greatly improved.
　-Teachers and students have bought into the idea that they can succeed.
　-A majority of the students have positive relationship with teachers.
　-Student scores have improved.
　-Student discipline has improved.
　-Student attendance has improved.
　-Teachers use engaging strategies instead of worksheet packets.
　-Learning actually takes place.

After reading this book you might have the impression that Lincoln High is a terrible place to work or go to school. The majority of my stories show the negative side of the school. This is only because the negative stories are more entertaining. I could write an equal number of stories about students experiencing success in class or completing group projects together without breaking out into a fight, but it wouldn't make for an interesting story.

Most schools in the country probably don't have a history of violence like LHS does, but LHS also has a history of success unlike most high schools. School violence was a phase and most of it is gone from the school. The community is still violent, but after our current students become part of the adult community it will slowly change. Eventually, the turnaround in the school could turn around the neighborhood and the city. When our current students have children that attend Lincoln they will hopefully be more prepared than their parents were.

Made in the USA
Charleston, SC
17 April 2016